Founded 19
The Story of The Newcastle Players

by
Geoff Price

First published 2006

Published
for
The Newcastle Players
by
Geoffrey H. Price
103 Paris Avenue
Newcastle, Staffs
ST5 2QP

Email: geoff.price63@ntlworld.com

© 2006 Geoffrey H. Price

Printed by
J. H. Brookes (Printers) Ltd.
Sneyd Green Business Park
Sneyd Street, Hanley
Stoke-on-Trent
Staffordshire
ST6 2NP

Introduction

When this project was conceived, it was intended to be a history of The Newcastle Players. As it proceeded, however, it became clear that a simple recital of all the plays the society had performed and the events that surrounded them would be rather tedious. In fact, when Eluned Mason was talking to Jo Rowley in a conversation about the early days recorded for our archives in 1983, she said, in response to Jo's question about why she was missing some plays out: "We're not going through all those. We'd have to go through about a hundred." That was over twenty years ago and we've done quite a few more plays since then.

I quickly realised that, rather than a history, stories about various aspects of The Newcastle Players would be more interesting. Then, having gathered them together, I realised that, as a whole, they made up *The Story of The Newcastle Players* from the society's inception in 1934 to the present day. And there's more to come.

There was discussion of a history of the society in the early 1980s and the minutes of an executive committee meeting in October 1983 record that Pat Mason agreed to ask his mother "to try to put together a 500 word history of the society to send to prospective new members."

A month later this was produced and, as a result, the committee "decided to ask Geoff Price to sit with Eluned and Jo Rowley and to tape any comments they may have on the background to the society and the past incidents, with a view to putting together a more detailed history."

In fact it was Eluned's grandson, Andrew, who recorded the conversation, which now exists on CD and in a transcription plus the notes (originally 1000 words long) written by Eluned prior to that.

So it could be said that this book has been at least twenty years in the making, although I've only been working on it seriously since early 2006 and it has ended up containing rather more than the 500 words that Eluned was originally asked for. Over 40,000 in fact.

Other sources I have used include:

- minutes of committee meetings over the years,

- scrapbooks kept by the Mason and Rowley families,

- programmes of all our productions

- press cuttings and other items kept for many years by Peter Tunstill and since Peter's death by myself

- and, in recent years, copies of the *Newcastle Players Bulletin*.

We also have in our archives:

- recordings of many, but not all, radio interviews broadcast by BBC Radio Stoke and Signal Radio,

- some recordings made at events such as our 40th Anniversary Party in 1974 plus

- two items from Ray Johnson's *Staffordshire Film Archive*.

I have found that people's memories – and my own for that matter – are not as accurate as they – and I – would like to think and where possible, therefore, I have sought confirmation – or otherwise – from written sources.

I am grateful to all who have contributed to this project, but particularly to my wife Mary who has patiently put up with the hours I have spent in my office – and elsewhere – ploughing through pages and pages of source material, not to mention my occasional excitement at discovering some hitherto forgotten but revealing fact. I am also greatly indebted to my son Richard for the considerable amount of time he spent converting my old photographs shot on film to digital images.

I would also like to thank Delyth Copp and Beryl Carter of Newcastle Borough Museum and Art Gallery for their help in tracing photographs of Newcastle and Staffordshire Sentinel Newspapers Limited for permission to use photographs of past productions.

CONTENTS

		Page
1.	The Early Years	1
2.	Marsh Street to Muni	6
3.	The Mitchell Memorial Theatre	16
4.	The Play's The Thing	28
5.	One-Act Plays and Other Performances	47
6.	Authors, Producers and Directors	53
7.	The Search for A Home of Our Own	57
8.	A Home of Our Own – The Newcastle Players Theatre Workshop	63
9.	. . . and Back to Marsh Street	72
10.	Anniversaries	74
11.	Ditties	85
12.	The Programmes	96
13.	Festivals and Awards	107
14.	Spreading A Word	110
15.	The Newcastle Players on Other Platforms	114
16.	The Newcastle Players and The Media	118
17.	Communicating with Our Members, Our Patrons and the Public at Large	123
18.	Newcastle Players People	132
19.	From Amateur to Professional	149
20.	Charity Ends Up At Home	157
21.	Presidential Postscript	160

APPENDICES

A.	Minutes of a General Meeting on 14th February 1937	165
B.	40th Anniversary Party – 17th January 1975	167
C.	Current members of the Newcastle Players	171
D.	Photo credits	173

1. The Early Years

Some details of the origins of the Newcastle Players are rather sketchy. We know that the society was founded in 1934 by John Rowley. We also know that our first production – *The Ghost Train* by Arnold Ridley – was presented at the Marsh Street Assembly Rooms, Newcastle in January 1935. But the only record we have of the first two years or so are copies of the play programmes and some press cuttings plus a printed list, probably dating from 1935, giving details of officers, patrons, the musicians in the "Players" String Quartette and members of the society.

The first records we have in the form of minutes of meetings are dated February 1937 (see Appendix A).

John Rowley's daughter Elizabeth – or Buffie as she is known to everybody – is our current President. Talking to local historian Mervyn Edwards for an article in the June 2003 issue of the *Sentinel* magazine *The Way We Were*, she said:

> My father John Rowley was interested in the theatre, but his mother thought it was a morally questionable world to enter. Our family being Catholic, my father started Newcastle Catholic Players who were connected to our church, Holy Trinity in London Road.
>
> He wanted to stage a play about someone being exorcised, but Father Kelly, the priest at Holy Trinity, felt this was unsuitable for the Catholic fraternity. My father tried to resolve the quarrel, but eventually started a new society called the Newcastle Players in 1934.

We have not been able to establish what the play in question was, but it would appear that, despite establishing a society that was no longer connected to Holy Trinity church – indeed our early productions were staged in premises belonging to the Methodist Church – we never actually performed that play. It certainly wasn't *The Ghost Train*.

During 1935 and 1936 four plays were presented at the Marsh Street Assembly Rooms (in what is now Merrial Street), Newcastle:

THE
NEWCASTLE PLAYERS

(Founded 1934)

President .. .. Dr. R. A. KEANE.
Chairman .. .. J. M. MASON, Esq.

Under the Distinguished Patronage of
HIS WORSHIP THE MAYOR (JOHN BENTLEY, Esq., J.P.).
THE DEPUTY MAYOR (ROBERT BERESFORD, Esq., J.P.).

W. T. Connelly, Esq.
Ernest Hartley, Esq.
J. R. Legge, Esq.
Bruce Maclean, M.D., M.R.C.P.
Wm. Mellard, Esq.
J. Moran, Esq., J.P.
M. S. O'Brien, Esq.
Ernest Rowley, Esq.
Mrs. John Rowley.
E. R. Taylor, Esq.
B. C. Tinsdill, Esq.
J. Wicks, Esq., A.I.S.A.

Hon. General Secretary:
Mr. J. G. WALSH,
"Kilbrogan," Southlands Avenue, Wolstanton, Staffs.

Hon Treasurer:
Mr. B. J. DEVANEY, "St. Mary's," Sutherland Drive,
Newcastle, Staffs.

Hon. Auditor:
Mr. J. WICKS, A.I.S.A., King Street, Newcastle.

"Players" String Quartette:

1st Violin .. .. .. H. Gumbley
2nd Violin .. .. Frank Coomer
'Cello .. .. .. J. Fallows
Pianoforte .. .. (Mrs.) B. Coupe

Members:

W. J. Hand, Rose Moran, J. Connelly C. Tinsdill J. Rowley,
D. Connelly, F. Frodsham, F. Hand, J. Frodsham, J. Emery,
G. Tindsill, N. Griffith, H. Barker, B. Robertson, J. W. Rowley,
J. Mason, J. Walsh, B. Devaney, M. Brown, M. Kent, F. Arnold,
M. Bourne, E. Bourne, M. Leeke, J. Wright, A. Leeke, W. Wright,
M. Fielding, P. Walsh, N. Robertson, P. Tams, F. Emery,
D. McKnight, M. Legge, M. Young, E. Young

- *The Ghost Train* by Arnold Ridley (January 1935)

- *The Barretts of Wimpole Street* by Rudolf Besier (November 1935)

- *Quality Street* by Sir James Barrie (March 1936) and

- *Interference* by Roland Pertwee & Harold Dearden (November 1936).

Extra performances of *The Ghost Train* were also given at Cotton College (17 February 1935) and the Town Hall, Stone (14 March 1935) and *The Barretts of Wimpole Street* at the Theatre Royal, Hanley (21 June 1936).

All these performances received critical acclaim:

> *The Ghost Train*: ... satisfying in every way. Mr. A. Ridley's three-act mystery play called for scenery and effects much more elaborate than are normally attempted on the amateur stage, and the producer Mr. John W. Rowley, is to be congratulated on his achievement and on the excellence of the team which was responsible for the various departments of the work behind the scenes.
>
> *The Barretts of Wimpole Street*: ... very finely interpreted by the Newcastle Players ... excellently staged and produced, and the success of the performance was due to all-round cooperation.
>
> *Quality Street*: ... enthusiastically received by a large audience ... fully up to the high standard of the Newcastle Players.
>
> *Interference*: ... interpretation by the Players was remarkably fine, team work assuring the building up of just the right atmosphere and individual ability giving conviction to each character.

Yet, while on the surface everything seemed to be running quite smoothly, there was an undercurrent of disagreement in the society which came to a head with the resignation of the Chairman, Jack Mason, and the Producer, John Rowley, at the end of 1936 or early 1937.

The sheet reproduced on the opposite page dates from 1935. It was presumably printed as an insert in the programme for "The Ghost Train". The reference to HIS WORSHIP THE MAYOR (John Bentley, Esq. J.P.) gives us a clue to the date, as Mr Bentley was Mayor from 1933 to 1935.

The cast of "The Barretts of Wimpole Street" (1935) and other members of the society.

Once again the problem was the choice of plays. It was alleged that one member in particular objected to five out of every six plays submitted for consideration. Commenting on the situation that arose, Jack Mason said at the time:

> No-one minds an objection here and there, but this wholesale rejection makes it very difficult ever to bring a selection of plays before the General Meeting. In spite of the fact that every modern play has been scrutinized with a zeal that would have delighted the Spanish Inquisition, by a miracle we have bridged the gap four times and produced four successful plays.

When it came to the fifth play, John Rowley as usual read twenty or thirty plays, which he whittled down to twelve for submission to the selection committee. The member who was the cause of all the trouble objected to at least eight of them After much discussion the list of possible plays was reduced to three: *Sweet Aloes* by Jay Mallory, *The Fake* by Frederick Lonsdale and *Turkey Time* by Ben Travers.

There were objections from the usual quarter to the first two: *Sweet Aloes* on moral grounds and *The Fake* because it was said that it condoned murder. However, the member in question suggested that the opinion of Father Kelly should be sought once again and it is alleged that he said: "If he (Father Kelly) passes them, I have no further objection."

In fact, although, Father Kelly said that he had no objection to *The Fake,* the dissenting member continued with his opposition to such an extent that Jack Mason and John Rowley felt that they could not go on.

The "old" Newcastle Players were disbanded and a general meeting attended by sixteen members was held on Sunday, 14th February 1937 (the minutes are reproduced in Appendix A) at which it was decided "that a Dramatic Society be formed and that Foundation members consist of those present together with any old members of the old "Newcastle Players" who apply within one Month."

Most of the officers elected were the same as before, minus the dissenting member of course. One significant change was the decision to admit non-Catholics as members – provided they were married to Catholic members. Eluned Mason, for example, was the wife of the Chairman and worked very hard for the society from the very beginning but, while she was allowed to provide "valued services" (as they are described in the programme for the 1936 production of *Quality Street*), as a non-Catholic she was not actually permitted to be a member until 1937.

Looking back on these events after forty or so years Eluned Mason said: "that was the only drama in the beginning. After that, the drama was all in plays."

It is perhaps worth mentioning that the first play following the formation of the "new" Newcastle Players was neither of those that had provoked the split but *The Two Mrs Carrolls*, a play by Martin Vale first produced at St Martin's Theatre, London in June 1935 and only recently released for amateur production. It again received critical acclaim, one reviewer starting his report with the following remarks:

> Coming after their two outstanding performances – "The Barretts of Wimpole Street" and "Interference" – the Newcastle Players could not have done any other than make this week's production of "The Two Mrs Carrolls" a brilliant success.

And from that time on we have gone in the words of John Legge (Chairman 1946 to 1952, President 1952 to 1963) "from strength to strength".

2. Marsh Street to Muni

Just before I started writing this book Mary and I took a holiday in Spain. In Catalunya to be exact. And in the coastal resort of Cambrils to be more exact.

During our stay the 47th Volta Ciclista de Tarragona took place. It involved 105 cyclists from 15 different teams covering a total distance of 693.5 kilometres over a period of five days. We took a particular interest in this event because one of the teams – the Football Club of Barcelona – was staying in the same hotel as us.

But was has this got to do with the Newcastle Players, you are probably wondering. Well. On the third day the cyclists rode from Cambrils to the neighbouring resort of Salou. It's four or five miles as the crow flies, but the cyclists took a roundabout route: 150 kilometres starting at half past three in the afternoon from Cambrils and getting to Salou three and a half hours later.

The history of the Newcastle Players is a bit like that. We started in Marsh Street (or Merrial Street as it's now called) in 1935 and fourteen years later we got to the Municipal Hall which was about 50 yards away in the Ironmarket. We took a roundabout route too: via Porthill and Priory Road.

In the programme for our Golden Jubilee production of *Outside Edge* in 1984 we rather grandly proclaimed, under the headline **50 Years – 5 Theatres,** that we had used four other theatres before moving to the Mitchell Memorial Theatre in 1958. To be accurate the Mitchell was the first true theatre. The first three venues were church halls and, rather oddly in view of the society's staunchly Catholic origins, none was attached to a Catholic church. One was Methodist and the other two Church of England. Although we referred to the fourth as The Municipal Hall Theatre, it was in fact a multi-purpose hall used for dances, flower shows, political meetings and a whole range of other events.

The Marsh Street Rooms

So, it all began at the Marsh Street Assembly Rooms in January 1935. The building is still there of course, but the street, which was once called Marsh Street at the east end and Merrial Street at the other, is now Merrial Street for

The Marsh Street Assembly Rooms photographed in 2006 from the police station doorway opposite.

the whole of its length. Also a plaque attached to the building by Newcastle-under-Lyme Civic Society in 2006 refers to it as Ebenezer School Rooms. The plaque is one of the first four attached by the Civic Society to landmark buildings to draw attention to their iconic status in the history of the town. It records that the building was originally erected in 1803 and rebuilt in 1822 and 1898, so it had been there for quite a few years when the Newcastle Players moved in.

By today's standards conditions at Marsh Street were far from ideal. Eluned Mason recalled that both men and women were huddled together in one dressing room for example. World War II also created some problems. The minutes of a committee meeting in November 1939 report that Mr Rowley stated "that the restrictions on Marsh St Rooms would be removed by the Police" but there is no explanation of what these restrictions were. The programmes for two plays at the time (*Nine Till Six* – November 1942 and *Yes and No* – February 1943) carried a note explaining that "In the exigencies of 'Black Out' the ventilation is not quite as adequate as is desired" and going on to "respectfully request" patrons "not to smoke to excess".

At the 1943 Annual General Meeting "Mr. Rowley reported on the play in progress, explaining why this was having to be proceeded with quickly on account of the difficulties existing appertaining to Marsh Street."

A scene from "Nine Till Six" at Marsh Street: (from left to right) Joy West, Adela Pickford, Clare Gatenby, Barbara Mason, Winifred Strachan and Enid Durrant.

These difficulties can be explained, but first it is necessary to explode a myth that has been current in the Newcastle Players for many years. Eluned Mason referred to it while reminiscing for the record in 1983 about our November 1942 production of *Nine Till Six*:

> The girls wore slit petticoats and Joe Sumberg lent us fur coats. It was an all-female cast and they were showing off these fur coats in the second act. They were running about downstairs – we were changing downstairs; the play was up a flight of stairs; and these girls were all running about in their petticoats. Then somebody came through the door and saw them and reported it. I don't really remember what happened, but we got sort of labelled as having an orgy. And all it was was a very simple, all-woman play. They couldn't wear frocks underneath. They were showing off fur coats. Soon after that we left Marsh Street.

More recently, in Ray Johnson's video tribute to Mary Blakeman (see page 135), Enid Frieder, who played Eluned's daughter in the production, recalled things slightly differently:

> Whoever it was that was in charge of the Methodist Hall came in when somebody was getting undressed onstage – and we only got down to pants and bras, which was terrible in those days, I suppose – and nearly fainted and had to be ushered out. And we were never allowed to set foot in the place again. And we were all girls together. But that was it and we were banished for ever from the Methodist Hall.

Far from being "never allowed to set foot in the place again" and "banished for ever" we went on to do another two plays there.

The reason we had to move on was that, owing to the national policy regarding Youth Movements, the Trustees of the Assembly Rooms were starting a Boys' Club and in consequence the premises would no longer be available to us. Later that year, in fact, the church authorities asked the Newcastle Players to conduct a play-reading class at the Youth Centre every week and various members, Mary Blakeman, Claire Gatenby, John Rowley and Fred Moreton, agreed to be available on a rota for this work.

St. Andrew's Hall, Porthill

In February 1944, six months after our last play in Marsh Street, we staged *Another Language* at St. Andrew's Hall in Porthill, followed in November of that year by *Hawk Island*. Those were the only two plays we did in Porthill and there was to be a two-year gap before we put on our next major production. The reason for this is not clear. Eluned Mason remembered that backstage conditions at Porthill left something to be desired:

> They'd got a stage and they'd got a little audience. I did noises off for one of the Porthill plays. There had to be a storm and we had to do the noises off in another room. It was most difficult. Bob Birkhead played the lead in both Porthill plays and there was this storm – thunder and lightning – going on over there and there was a little passage and I was shut in here with a wind machine doing this and then I'd got a sort drum affair which I was making thunder with. Oh, it was hair-raising.

A two-year break

Whatever the reason, the only play we produced between November 1944 and November 1946 was a one-act play (*The Bride* by Gertrude Jennings) presented to a members-only audience in our rehearsal room for one performance on Thursday, 26 July 1945. Enid Durrant, later to be Enid Tunstill and now Enid Frieder, was a member of the all-women cast.

Though no plays were produced during this period, it was the start of a time of strenuous activity seeking a home of our own. But that is the subject of a separate chapter.

St. Giles' Parish Hall

Productions resumed in November 1946 with *Ladies in Retirement* at St. Giles Parish Hall, at the bottom of Priory Road in Newcastle. We put on five plays there in as many years.

St Giles Parish Hall photographed in 2006. The building, which was for many years the home of an advertising agency, now houses a chiropractic clinic.

Eluned Mason recalled that it had a very small stage: "Very cramped," she said:

> In *No Medals* (the last play we did there, in January/February 1949 – GHP) it was very difficult, when the men all came in and I had to lay a breakfast table. We were all having poached eggs for breakfast and I opened a tin of apricots and put an apricot on a piece of dried bread as a poached egg. But by the time I'd laid the table and everybody had come in for breakfast there was no room for anybody else there.

A scene from "No Medals" at St Giles Parish Hall: (from left to right) Harold Vernon, Ben Devall, Enid Tunstill, John D. Steventon, Peter Tunstill, Alan Spriggs and Joe Bunch.

In spite of the cramped stage there were two different scenes in *No Medals*: The sitting room of a furnished house to start with and then, for the second half of the play, the quayside as seen in the photograph above.

Another problem was that anyone having to go offstage on one side and come back in on the other had to go outside and walk – or even run sometimes – around the back of the building to get back in. "That was perfectly all right if you had time," Eluned said, "but very difficult if it was wet." There were umbrellas, of course, but the umbrellas always seemed to be on the wrong side. "Two of the nights (in one play) were wet and it was dreadful" which strikes me as being something of an understatement.

St. Giles was the scene of an incident, also involving Eluned, which has become part of Newcastle Players folklore:

For *Autumn* (December 1947) a piano was required to be played offstage. Unfortunately, the stage had no wing space but there was a sort of shelf eight feet or so up in the air and this was where the piano was located. Also, the only way the pianist – Eluned Mason – could get there was to climb up a ladder and over the top of the set before the play started. What's more, once there she had to stay there for the whole evening.

One night, the cast and other members of the society were relaxing in the pub after the show when Pat Mason suddenly exclaimed: "Where's my mother?" You've guessed it. She was still on her shelf, patiently waiting for someone to remember her, to switch the lights back on and to come to her rescue.

Recalling the incident Eluned said: "They all went off and left me there. I kept saying: 'Don't go! I'm here! I want a ladder. I can't get down.' But I did get down." Maybe she'd forgotten that they came back from the pub for her.

The fifth play we did at St. Giles' was *No Medals* by Esther McCracken (January 1949) and then later that year we moved to Municipal Hall in the Ironmarket, Newcastle.

The Municipal Hall Theatre

The move to the Municipal Hall provided more space for actors and audience alike. It was a magnificent building in many ways, but it was still not a real theatre. The stage had no proper proscenium, just an oversized pelmet with floor-length drapes to the left and right. There was a kitchen stage-right and, if the door was not kept shut – sometimes even if it was – the clatter of cups and saucers could distract from the action on stage.

The foundation stone for the Municipal Hall was laid on 6th July 1888 by Henry Coghill, Esq., J.P., a prominent local businessman and a major subscriber to the building fund, who gave £1,000 towards the total cost of £18,000. The red brick building was opened on 14th October 1890 and demolished in 1967. During its comparatively short life it housed council offices, the School of Art and the public library. The catalogue for an exhibition entitled "Lost Buildings of Newcastle" at Newcastle Museum in 1995 described how a magnificent staircase led from the ground floor entrance hall to "an assembly room with stage and orchestra area". This was used as a theatre by the Newcastle Players and other groups, amateur and professional.

This room had the potential to seat a much bigger audience than we had been able to cater for previously. The first three halls we used had a capacity of

The Municipal Hall, Ironmarket, Newcastle-under-Lyme. The building behind the curve in the wall is the police station which is on the opposite side of the street to what we knew as the Marsh Street Assembly Rooms.

The Municipal Hall stage during the demolition work in the late sixties. The doorway on the left of the picture led directly into the kitchen.

between 200 and 250. The Muni, on the other hand, could seat over 400. Unfortunately all the seats were on the flat and not all of them had a good view of stage which gave rise to a stream of complaints from our patrons.

Although, unlike Marsh Street and Porthill, there were separate dressing rooms for men and women, they were just two long thin triangular spaces up two spiral staircases from the stage. In *Viceroy Sarah* (November 1952) the female members of the cast found these almost impossible to negotiate in their voluminous dresses and period hairstyles. Fortunately, as Eluned Mason recalled, someone found an unlocked room elsewhere in the building and they used that.

But that was not all. Throughout the time we were at the Municipal Hall we had constant problems. Equipment often did not work or was missing. There were occasions when we were charged for the use of equipment which was non-existent. And time and again we had difficulty booking the hall in the first place. The reason for this appears to have been the council's reluctance to allow the hall to be used for week-long lets in case it prevented it being used

Eluned Mason and Olive Wright in their voluminous "Viceroy Sarah" dresses at the Municipal Hall. Also in the picture are Peter Upton (left) and Jeremy Smith.

on one night for a dance or a flower show or a jumble sale. Meetings were held on several occasions with the Borough Treasurer and the Chairman of the Estates Committee to try to resolve the situation, but in the end we started to look elsewhere.

Alternative solutions that were considered included moving to the Victoria Hall at Kidsgrove, going back to the hall in Priory Road, even acquiring a building we could convert into a theatre of our own. But that is the subject of another chapter. Against this backdrop of continual obstacles, though, we managed to present a total of nineteen plays at the Municipal Hall between October 1949 and April 1958, most of them produced by Mary Blakeman.

Finally though the decision was taken – after much soul-searching about leaving the borough – to move to the Mitchell Memorial Theatre, Hanley which we did in November 1958. And that too is the subject of another chapter.

3. The Mitchell Memorial Theatre

In the programme for our Golden Jubilee production of *Outside Edge* in 1984 I wrote:

> To many regular members of our audience it may come as a surprise to learn that we have not always performed at the Mitchell Memorial Theatre. For one thing, when the society was established fifty years ago, this theatre had not been thought of, let alone built. For another, although we have looked upon the Mitchell as our stage home for the last twenty-six years, we used four other halls, all in Newcastle as it happens, before finally settling here.

That was over twenty years ago and we are still at The Mitch. No other group has used the theatre for anything like as long as the Newcastle Players. And yet our tenure has not always been secure. The main reason for that is that the official title of the building was, and still is, "The Mitchell Memorial Youth Centre" and we are classed as an adult group.

The Mitchell Memorial Theatre was officially opened on 28th October 1957 by Group Captain Douglas Bader. It had been suggested as early as 1940 that the City of Stoke-on-Trent should erect a building as a memorial to Reginald Mitchell, a native of the city and the designer of the Spitfire fighter aircraft which had played a decisive role in the Battle of Britain. Various ideas were considered and the one adopted, for a youth centre, was put forward by Mr. J. F. Carr, the City's then Director of Education.

An appeal to raise £100,000 was launched by the Lord Mayor of Stoke-on-Trent, Alderman C. Austin Brook, on Sunday, 28 February 1943, at a special showing at the Regent Cinema in Hanley of *The First of the Few*, the film dramatization of the life and work of Reginald Mitchell. Financial contributions were made by companies, organisations of various kinds, schools and private individuals, not only locally but also from other parts of the country and from as far afield as America and Australia, but by the opening day the fund had only reached £70,000, not the hoped-for £100,000. The building itself cost more than £50,000 and £20,000 had been made available to Southampton, where Reginald Mitchell had died, to establish engineering scholarships.

The Mitchell Memorial Theatre photographed during our run of "Because of the Lockwoods" in April 2006.

A report at the time of the opening stated that "though, due to financial considerations, the facilities do not quite match the ambitions of the original conception, the Mitchell Memorial Theatre and Youth Centre is a fitting memorial to one of North Staffordshire's most distinguished sons". And it added that the administration and maintenance of the building would now be the responsibility of the local education authority. The centre was intended to stimulate interest in a wide range of subjects throughout the city, and particularly in the sphere of youth and community work. Drama, music, speech training, public speaking, film appreciation and dancing were among the courses it was proposed to run. Drama festivals and individual productions would be encouraged.

It is interesting to read that, when opened, the three storey building provided "on the first floor a lecture room with accommodation for 80 people and three dressing rooms which can be used for meetings on a smaller scale, a well-proportioned foyer, first-floor tea bar and another tea bar for the actors on the top floor". In fact the top floor tea bar and the third dressing room are but distant memories, having been converted many years ago to office space.

Unlike any of the halls we had performed in on a regular basis in the previous twenty or so years, the Mitchell was a real theatre with a stage 24 feet deep plus an apron, wing space, proper stage curtains, a proscenium arch 28 feet wide by 12 feet high, lighting, raked seating suitable for a potential audience of 380 and so on. Although we had some reservations about moving from Newcastle, the problems we were having with the Municipal Hall seemed to outweigh our reservations and so we started to investigate a move to the new theatre.

All was not plain sailing though. Our Executive Committee first discussed the possible move on 24th October 1957, a week before the theatre was officially opened, and a decision was made to make enquiries at once. There was some initial correspondence with the theatre after which we enquired if the theatre would be available to us for the week 16th to 23rd November 1958 (Sunday to Sunday). We also asked about the possibility of two permanent bookings – one in March and one in November.

The response was that our request could not be considered before the meeting of the Education Committee in May. However, this was brought forward slightly and at the meeting of the City of Stoke-on-Trent Further Education Sub-Committee held on 14th April 1958 a resolution was passed that a number of lettings should be approved. Item (vii) under this heading was:

> Newcastle Players: That in principle it be agreed that lettings be made during the coming year and that consideration be given to applications for succeeding years.

At the August 1958 Executive Committee meeting the Secretary reported that the cost of hiring the Mitchell Memorial Theatre for the week would be £53 plus the cost of the service of the fireman/electrician. This would cover the use of the theatre, two dressing rooms, two kitchens, box office, cloakroom, foyer and public tea bar. There would be an additional charge at the rate of 7/- per hour while the fireman/electrician, Mr Ray Martin, was on the premises which was likely to be three hours per night. Any Sunday time would also be charged at 7/- per hour. Mr Martin would request the stage manager to sign his attendance sheet each day to substantiate his services to us.

A scene from our 1958 production of "The House by the Lake": (left to right) Marion Wordsworth, Eluned Mason, John Talbot, Patricia Bentley, Denis Connelly, Alan Spriggs, Margaret Hargreaves, Ray Backes and Vida Stevens.

On that basis we moved to the Mitchell Memorial Theatre in November 1958 and opened on Wednesday, 26th with Mary Blakeman's production of *The House by the Lake* by Hugh Mills.

The programme for *The House by the Lake* contained a note explaining the change of venue:

> THE Newcastle Players would be unable to function as a society without the excellent support from you our patrons. It is only natural therefore that your welfare and comfort should be of primary interest to us and whilst we all regret leaving Newcastle we are presenting our plays at the Mitchell Memorial Theatre, Hanley, in the future, because it is ideally suited to us and offers greater comfort and facilities for you.
>
> We sincerely believe that you will benefit from our move and trust that it will be justified by your continued support.

At the society's Annual General Meeting the following February the President spoke of the great success we had achieved from moving to the Mitchell Memorial Youth Centre in Hanley although everyone regretted having to leave Newcastle. And later that year we proudly announced in our programme for *Witness for the Prosecution*:

Now we have moved to this delightful theatre we have more room backstage and use of the workshops at the rear can be obtained for scenery design. In view of this improved position it is the intention of the Society to reorganise our scenery production section with a view to producing our own sets in time for the Autumn play next year.

In 1961, after using the name Mitchell Memorial Theatre, as we do now, it would appear that we were reminded by the City Education Department that the building was officially a youth centre and we were required to use the name Mitchell Memorial Youth Centre Theatre, which we did for the next twenty years.

In the mid-sixties our euphoria became somewhat muted, since demand for the theatre's facilities from youth groups, who did not have to pay for using it, resulted in the three adult societies, which used it and also paid for the privilege, finding it difficult to get bookings. This situation was discussed at some length at our Annual General Meeting in March 1965 as summarised in the minutes:

> The President, John Barstow, spoke of our problem at the Mitchell Memorial Youth Centre Theatre and said that sooner or later the adult societies would not be able to perform there since the demand for the theatre was being taken up more and more by youth clubs. We had, however, approached the Town Clerk and had an encouraging response. Our efforts towards finding some other suitable theatre were well in hand and we were working very closely with the Arnold Bennett Theatre Committee on which the Newcastle Players have four members attending regularly. This committee was also in the process of negotiating with the Town Clerk and various buildings in the district are being viewed but none are really suitable. However, all these developments and the reports in the press might give us a chance of moving towards a theatre.
>
> The Vice-President, Denis Connelly who had been on the sub-committee to deal with the MMT bookings had not a happy report to make. He said there were three main societies using the MMT, namely the New Era Players, the New Intimate Theatre and the Newcastle Players, who required a minimum of six dates per year, that is three in the spring and three in the autumn. The Education Authority only offered five and these were not good dates. After a lot of discussion and sorting out it was agreed that the New Intimate and the Newcastle Players should toss a coin for the last date and it resulted in our getting two bad dates for 1965 namely May and December. We pleaded with the MMT people who claimed and with just justification that the accent

must be on youth. Mr Connelly then said that that the dates generally were not being allocated properly – but they could try and approach bookings sensibly if they wished. There was an urgent need for something to be done to find alternative accommodation and this was why the Arnold Bennett Theatre Project was formed. Things were moving in the right direction even if slowly. The Arnold Bennett Committee had prepared a most comprehensive schedule of the requirements of all the organisations affiliated to it and it had been sent to the Town Clerk in July 1964. But to date they had received no reply. At the Newcastle Players last production the President was approached by a certain local Alderman was suggested that we might approach the Town Clerk and this we had done and it did appear to have revived things. A circular about accommodation had been sent by the local authority to all local societies. There was far more talk today of the needs of amateur drama than there had been for some time and the more we talked about it the more chance we had for success but he closed with the warning that we should anticipate difficulty during 1966.

The Arnold Bennett Memorial Theatre project had arisen as early 1963 at the suggestion of the New Era Players as a result of the difficulties they had experienced in booking the Mitchell. The idea gathered momentum and was supported all the adult drama societies in North Staffordshire including the North Staffordshire Drama Association with its 24 affiliated societies. The chairman of the Arnold Bennett Theatre Committee was Roy Shaw, Director of Extramural Studies at the University of Keele, who was later to be the Secretary-General of the Arts Council of Great Britain.

In the course of 1963 there was considerable debate in the pages of the *Evening Sentinel* to which our then President, John Barstow, contributed the following comments:

> On behalf of the Newcastle Players I offer the very strongest support for a "Little Theatre" and if this can take the form of an Arnold Bennett memorial I am sure support would be forthcoming from many Five Towns enthusiasts.
>
> In the meanwhile, since these projects take a long time to fructify, I would ask that the trustees of the Mitchell Memorial Youth Centre and the committee responsible for the letting of the Mitchell Theatre to give their kindest consideration to applications for renting from societies such as mine in order that they can continue their activities which have been proved so popular.
>
> This is of vital importance in an area where facilities for amateurs are so limited.

Discussion continued throughout 1964 but the idea of an alternative to the Mitchell seemed to be making progress in 1965 when Alderman Horace Barks, Chairman of the City Libraries and Museums Committee, stated: "Stoke-on-Trent will have a new civic theatre built in the next three years." It would have a conventional proscenium stage; it would seat an audience in the region of 300-350; and it would be included in the proposed extensions to the City Museum. However, the Town Clerk expressed the view that Mr Barks might have been a little too enthusiastic.

There were immediately adverse comments that a theatre of the size suggested would be of no use whatever to the operatic societies and *Screamline*, the Scouts' gang show. At least one correspondent wrote to the *Evening Sentinel* to ask: "Do the councillors and amateurs really want a small 'intimate' type of theatre appealing only to intellectual highbrows (and snobs)?"

Among the letters reacting to this view was another from John Barstow who wrote:

> My society have not produced one single play that could possibly he called highbrow. Amateurs do not kid themselves – they take pleasure in providing good entertainment for a number of regular theatre-goers, who deplore the absence of top professional productions, and my society plays to 85 per cent full houses. It is in consideration of this that the city councillors are contemplating the provision of an intimate theatre to meet this demand. How futile it would be for them even to consider a larger project at this stage.

While all this was going we were looking at alternatives. A small committee consisting of Ray Backes, Peter Tunstill and Bill Stevens visited the Queen's Hall, the Princes Hall, the Lecture Hall and the Jubilee Hall but, in their opinion, the only hall that could possibly be considered was the Jubilee Hall. Even that had many deficiencies in that there was a very low stage, no toilet facilities within reach of the cast, no stage lighting and the stage was so low that there might be difficulty in seeing from the rear of the hall.

In October 1965 John Abberley, who was then the theatre correspondent of the *Evening Sentinel*, suggested in his weekly column *On stage* that the more economical solution would be to scrap the civic theatre project, turn the Mitchell centre over to purely theatrical activities and build a new youth centre.

In the event the city council went on to convert the Queen's Hall in Burslem into a sort of theatre and later on, with the assistance of National Lottery

A scene from "Celebration" (April 1966): (left to right) Marjorie Griffiths, John Harwood, Bob West, Mary Blakeman and John Talbot. The play was produced by Ray Backes.

funding, converted the Regent Cinema into a showpiece theatre – both far too big for the sort of productions present by the Newcastle Players.

As far as we were concerned our worries of the previous couple of years or so appeared to go away with the news that our bookings for 1966 had been confirmed as the week commencing 17th April and week commencing 20th November with plus Saturday 17th September for an evening of one-act plays. Everyone felt that all the efforts that had been made had at last borne fruit and we could only hope that our stay at the Mitchell would continue to our advantage.

Our production that April was, perhaps rather appropriately, *Celebration* by Keith Waterhouse and Willis Hall, of which the *Evening Sentinel* reviewer wrote, under the headline **Newcastle comedy one of best half dozen in 10 years**:

> In almost a decade of reviewing several hundred plays, I have found fewer than half a dozen amateur productions which have succeeded in

really creating the basic element of illusion which is an integral part of good theatre.

Last night, I am delighted to say, I was able to add another to my select list – Newcastle Players' production of "Celebration".

Roy Shaw described it (see letter on the opposite page) as "the best argument I have heard for a long time for a purpose-built theatre for amateur productions".

Although we have stayed at the Mitchell ever since, attempts have been made to lure us away to other venues: there was talk of converting Friarswood School in Newcastle into a small theatre, but that never came to fruition; we were invited to view the Queen's Theatre in Burslem, but it was far to big for our requirements; and perhaps the most persistent suitor was former Lord Mayor of Stoke-on-Trent, Sir Harold Clowes, who had been instrumental in setting up what he like to call a "Theatre in the Suburbs" in the community hall named after him at Bentilee.

When it opened in 1957 the Mitchell Memorial Theatre was under the control of Stoke-on-Trent City Council. With the reorganisation of local government in 1974 it passed to Staffordshire County Council and then in due course at the next reorganization it went back to Stoke-on-Trent. But it was not until 2005 that the council established a non-executive regulatory committee "to assume the function of decision-making in relation to the Trust known as The Mitchell Memorial Youth Centre".

The committee's terms of reference were to act within the constitution and charitable objectives of the Centre, and in accordance with the Scheme made under the Charities Act 1960 and the general law. It was anticipated that it would meet infrequently, the day-to-day management of the Centre and its staff remaining the responsibility of the Director of Education and Lifelong Learning. However, it was intended that future reports to the committee would consider the various options for the future management of the Centre.

At the committee's inaugural meeting in June 2005 its chairman, Councillor Peter Kent-Bagguley, described the Mitchell building as a "gem of a resource", accepting that "we have, therefore, an enormous duty of care, to ensure that the fabric of the building is maintained to the highest standards".

One of the first tasks the committee tackled was the question of rental charges. The Newcastle Players have always paid for the use of the theatre and over the

Department of Extramural Studies
University of Keele

KEELE   STAFFORDSHIRE

Director: Roy Shaw, BA

Telephone: Keele Park 313/4

21st April 1966

Dear Mr Tunstill,

    I must write and thank you for my evening's enjoyment on Tuesday.

    It was quite the best amateur performance I have seen for a very long time, and better than some professional performances I have seen. The sets were splendid, the direction superb, and the performance from almost everybody was quite remarkable. So excellent a team was it that it would be quite invidious to pick out individuals; I will only say that your young players surprisingly managed to hold up the level of the performance to the high standards set by your experienced senior members.

    This production is the best argument I have heard for a long time for a purpose-built theatre for amateur productions.

    With renewed thanks, and every good wish to you all.

                    Yours sincerely,

                    Roy Shaw
                    Director of Extramural Studies

Mr F.A. Tunstill,
Blithe Cottage,
29 Tavistock Crescent,
Newcastle, Staffs

years the amount involved had risen from the original £53 to something approaching £1000 per week. Some groups, which needed more dressing room space because of the size of their casts, were reportedly paying nearer £2000 per week. On the other hand, groups affiliated to the Youth and Community Service originally paid nothing at all and had the free run of the centre, whereas we could only use the rooms we had booked during the hours we paid for.

In 1999 it was announced that the affiliated groups would have to pay £50 per week in future and this amount went up to £75 a few years later. In 2006, however, Councillor Kent-Bagguley told the Mitchell Memorial Theatre User Group that his committee was planning to rectify the inequality of the theatre's current charging policy which allowed some groups to pay only £75 for a week's use of all the theatre's facilities, while others are charged vastly more.

The proposal, which became a reality in April 2006, was to classify users into two categories: (a) not-for-profit organisations and (b) individuals or commercial organisations. Within these two categories there would be two sub-categories: organisations with the majority of users under 20 years old and organisations with the majority of users over 20 years old. Newcastle Players is a not-for-profit organisation with the majority of users over 20 years old. The new charges did not adversely affect us, but most of the groups, which had previously paid much less than us while enjoying greater use of the facilities, complained bitterly about what they saw as the injustice of the new charges.

That reminds me of an incident reported to us some years ago. Apparently one of the "free" groups complained to the then manager of the Mitchell about the Newcastle Players being allowed to clear the stage on the Sunday morning after a production whereas they had to vacate the theatre on the Saturday night. "There's obviously one rule for them and another for people like us," they added. "Certainly there is," replied the manager. "They pay and you don't. Would you like to change over to their terms?" You can guess the answer.

Another change to our advantage was with the formation of the Mitchell Memorial Theatre User Group. Prior to 2004 there had been a committee called the Stoke-on-Trent Drama Development Committee, which comprised only groups affiliated to Youth and Community Centres that used the Mitchell Memorial Theatre. As such, in spite of having used the theatre longer than any other group, we were not eligible for membership and, therefore, had no say in the way the theatre operated. But, when the user group came into existence, we were able to join and I think we have been able to make a valuable contribution. At the same time, the rules of the Mitchell Memorial Theatre Full-Length Play Festival were changed and we became eligible for that too, but that is dealt with in another chapter.

There have been other changes over the years. When we first started using the theatre it was fully equipped with lighting and sound equipment, there was a resident electrician/fireman and refreshments for the audience in the interval were provided by members of Stoke-on-Trent Youth Council. The latter service was withdrawn in 1977. Since 1997 we have had to hire the services of outside lighting and sound contractors, and we now have to provide our own fire officer in addition to the other front-of-house staff specified in the conditions of rental.

There have also been changes in the seating capacity of the theatre. Originally there was a total of 380 seats, although we have always reserved the back row for the use of members on duty, leaving 369 for sale to our patrons. Later three seats were earmarked for the use of a fire steward and Red Cross attendants which brought the total down to 366. When musicals were presented at the theatre, the first two rows of the centre block would be removed and, after a time, it was decided to remove these permanently, making the capacity 342. Then, in 2005, four seats at each end of row P in the centre block were removed to provide space for wheelchairs. So the capacity of the theatre is now 338 provided there are four wheelchair users present.

4. The Play's The Thing

Ask any six members of the Newcastle Players what their favourite play is and you will get six different answers. And if you stand at the back of the theatre as the audience leaves at the end of the performance, you are bound to hear at least one person say: "It's the best you've ever done".

When Eluned Mason and Jo Rowley were chatting for the record in 1983, they were obviously looking through their scrapbooks and comparing notes on different productions but at one point Eluned remarked that they could go through them all. "We'd have go through about a hundred plays", she said.

That was over twenty years ago. We have now performed over 120 full length plays and nearly 70 one-act plays, some of both types more than once, so I don't intend to discuss every play we have ever done in detail, but some are worth more of a closer look than others.

Marsh Street Assembly Rooms – 1935 to 1943

We did fifteen plays (one of them twice) at Marsh Street at a rate of two a year except in 1939 and 1942, when presumably wartime conditions created problems. Certainly the shortage of men was responsible for the choice of the all-women play *Nine Till Six* in 1942.

All these plays were produced by John Rowley and in many of them, particularly in the thirties, he played a leading role.

There is no doubt that we got off to a good start with *The Ghost Train*. The favourable press comment that this and other early productions received has already been quoted in chapter one.

The Marsh Street plays were:

The Ghost Train	*Quality Street*
by Arnold Ridley	by Sir J. M. Barrie
The Barretts of Wimpole Street	*Interference*
by Rudolf Besier	by Roland Pertwee & Harold Dearden

A scene from "I Have Five Daughters" at Marsh Street in July 1943: (left to right) Adela Pickford, Pat Dawson, Joy West, Barbara Mason and Peggy Moreton

The Two Mrs. Carrolls
by Martin Vale

Distinguished Gathering
by James Parish

Bird in Hand
by John Drinkwater

The Wind and the Rain
by Merton Hodge

Murder on the Second Floor
by Frank Vosper

Children to Bless You
by G. Sheila Donisthorpe

Quiet Wedding
by Esther McCracken

Dear Octopus
by Dodie Smith

Nine Till Six
by Aimee & Philip Stuart

Yes and No
by Kenneth Horne

I Have Five Daughters
by Margaret MacNamara

The Ghost Train and *The Barretts of Wimpole Street* were performed for three nights each. Then, until 1941, the run increased to four or five nights, after which it was six, seven or, in the case of *I Have Five Daughters* in 1943, eight nights starting on Friday 23rd July and continuing until Saturday 31st July.

The play that we did twice, first in April 1938 and again in January 1940, was *Bird in Hand*. The second performance was in aid of Red Cross Supplies and Newcastle Nursing Association. There were three cast changes: Doreen McKnight, Harry Oakes and John Mason were replaced by Vida Stevens (incorrectly listed as Vida Stephens in the programme), Harold Hayden and John Barstow. The furniture probably looked the same as it was provided by J. C. Grealy of Newcastle on both occasions, but the set was presumably different as the first came from Manchester and the second from Newcastle. This performance was also repeated for one night only a week or so later at Crewe Theatre in aid of the Crewe Red Cross Fund.

Other one-night stands away from Marsh Street included *The Ghost Train* at Cotton College, the catholic boys school at Oakamoor, on 17th February 1935 and Stone Town Hall on 14th March 1935; The *Barretts of Wimpole Street* at the Theatre Royal, Hanley on 21st June 1936 in aid of the North Staffs Royal Infirmary £20,000 Radium Appeal; and *Yes and No* at the Grand Theatre, Leek on 7th March 1943 in aid of the Leek & District Prisoners of War Fund.

There is no record of how much the charity performances raised, but the society's action on behalf of the Infirmary appeal was widely applauded in the press. There was, however, one dissenting voice. Someone writing to the Editor of the *Sentinel* and using the pen name NEWCASTLE expressed amazement "that the Newcastle Players are to give a performance on Sunday, June 21st – the Lord's Day, of all days." A reply from ANOTHER NEWCASTILIAN quoted scriptural authority for such humanitarian action on the Sabbath and concluded by saying:

> So far from injuring the cause of the Sunday performance, I hope the letter of "Newcastle" will decide larger numbers to support the Infirmary effort by being present at the performance, and that they will reward the Newcastle Players by supporting the future productions given on their own account.

The Crewe and Leek performances were also on Sunday, but there is no record of any protest.

"Another Language" at Porthill in February 1944: (left to right) Eluned Mason, Eric Ash, Sydney Durrant, Winifred Strachan, Peter Tunstill, Vida Stevens, John Rowley, Robert Birkhead, Claire Gatenby, Joan Connelly and Fred Moreton.

St Andrew's Hall, Porthill – 1944

We only spent one year at Porthill and did two plays there: *Another Language* by Rose Franken adapted by Moncton Hoffe and *Hawk Island* by Howard Irving Young.

Between these we made a trip in July to the Congregational Church Hall, Chesterton for two performances of *Yes and No* in aid of the Chesterton & Red Street Prisoners-of-War Comforts Fund. The cast was exactly the same as at Marsh Street in February of the previous year.

The Fallow Period – 1945 and 1946

Between November 1944 and November 1946 we were without a theatrical home and we gave no public performances, but we did do a one-act play by Gertrude Jennings for a members-only audience. A recreation of the programme is reproduced overleaf. The type on the original copies in our archives is too faded to reproduce clearly.

Programme

"THE BRIDE"

A Comedy in One Act
by
Gertrude Jennings

Newcastle Players Rehearsal Room
Thursday, 26th July, 1945

The Cast

Mrs Irving	Enid Durrant
Joyce	Pat Dawson
Judith	Joan Moreton
Susan (The Maid)	Peggy Moreton
Madame Grace	Winifred Strachan
Miss Sparrow	Olive Wright

Stage Manager	William Stevens
Prompt	Margaret Moreton
Properties	(Winifred Strachan
	(Olive Wright

Production – John W. Rowley

Scene - Bedroom of a house in Onslow Square
Time - The present. About 1.30 p.m.

Silver Collection

A scene from "The Blue Goose" at the Priory Hall in April 1948: (left to right) Harold Vernon, Winifred Glover, Mary Blakeman, Enid Tunstill, Joan Moreton, Stanley Thirlwall and Vida Stevens.

St Giles Parish Hall – 1946 to 1949

We did five plays at the Parish Hall (also known as the Priory Hall), all for six nights:

Autumn
by Margaret Kennedy
& Gregory Ratoff

Ladies in Retirement
by Edward Percy
& Reginald Denham

Winter Sunshine
by G. A. Thomas

The Blue Goose
by Peter Blackmore

No Medals
by Esther McCracken

This period saw the start of Mary Blakeman's long and didtinguished production career with the Newcastle Players. In *Ladies in Retirement* Mary both acted and produced the play under the direction of John Rowley. Regrettably there are no photographs of this production in our archives. She again was producer under John Rowley's direction for *Winter Sunshine*. She produced *Autumn* on her own and John produced *The Blue Goose* while Mary played the role of Mrs Elizabeth Portal. It was to be the last play John produced.

The Municipal Hall – 1949 to 1958

We presented nineteen plays at the Municipal Hall, each for four nights: fewer performances than we had been giving in recent years at our previous venues, but this hall had a bigger seating capacity:

Jupiter Laughs
by A. J. Cronin

Pink String and Sealing Wax
by Roland Pertwee

Badger's Green
by R. C. Sherriff

Bonaventure
by Charlotte Hastings

The Happiest Days of Your Life
by John Dighton

Home at Seven
by R. C. Sherriff

Viceroy Sarah
by Norman Ginsbury

Castle in the Air
by Alan Melville

Wind of Heaven
by Emlyn Williams

The Hollow
by Agatha Christie

After My Fashion
by Diana Morgan

His Excellency
by Dorothy & Campbell Christie

Down Came a Blackbird
by Peter Blackmore

Relative Values
by Noël Coward

Book of the Month
by Basil Thomas

Sabrina Fair
by Samuel Taylor

A Question of Fact
by Wynyard Browne

Red Letter Day
by Andrew Rosenthal

Spider's Web
by Agatha Christie

Mary Blakeman produced the majority of these, but three (*Bonaventure, Castle in the Air* and *A Question of Fact*) were produced by Alan Spriggs. Mary Blakeman had acting roles in *Bonaventure* and *A Question of Fact*.

Vida Stevens and Denis Connelly in "Castle in the Air" (above) and Margaret Jones, Michael Owens, Alan Spriggs, Ray Backes, Denis Connelly, Enid Tunstill, Monty Slater and John Talbot in "Spider's Web" (below).

The Mitchell Memorial Theatre – 1958 to the present day

Our productions at the Mitchell fall into two categories: full-length plays, which are our main productions, and evenings of one-act plays and, sometimes, other items. The latter will be dealt with in a subsequent chapter.

In the nearly fifty years we have been at the Mitch we have performed 91 full-length plays. The full list is at the end of this chapter. It is in alphabetical order, as nine of the plays have been performed twice: four were repeats of plays we had done previously in Newcastle (*Bonaventure, Ladies in Retirement, Relative Values* and *The Ghost Train*) and five at the Mitchell at intervals varying between 19 and 40 years: *The House by the Lake (*1958 & 1998), *My Three Angels (*1959 & 1981), *Suddenly at Home (*1977 & 1999), *Not Now Darling (*1979 & 1998) and *How the Other Half Loves (*1981 & 2005).

There was usually a complete change of cast between the two productions but there were exceptions. Enid Tunstill played Felicity, Countess of Marchwood, both times in *Relative Values:* she was thirty years too young for the part the first time, but the right age when the play was revived in 1985. John Talbot was Jules (6817) in the two versions of *My Three Angels.* Mary Blakeman was in both productions of *Ladies in Retirement* but playing a different part, as were Bob and Di West in *Not Now Darling.*

Since 1959 we have generally staged two full-length plays at the Mitch each year, one in the spring and the other in the autumn. But there were exceptions.

In August 1976 we announced that our next production (in November) would be *Suddenly at Home* by Francis Durbridge, but it was not to be. They say that misfortunes come in threes and that was certainly the case with this production. Originally Jackie Davies was to have played Helen Tenby, but she was taken ill and Vida Stephens took over the part. Then Vida was injured in a car crash on her way to a rehearsal. We did not have a replacement within our own ranks but we knew that June Hodson had played the part fairly recently in a Studio One production, so we approached her and she agreed to do it, but almost immediately she had to drop out because her husband was taken ill.

The play was postponed until April 1977 when it went on with Vida in the jinxed part and most of the rest of the cast unchanged. Even then the gremlins struck again, as the *Evening Sentinel* put it, for Vida was stricken with

Vida Stevens (third right) in our 1977 production of "Suddenly at Home". Also in the picture (from left to right) are Di West, Doug Challinor, Edward Crew, Richard Stevens and Ann Hurlstone.

laryngitis. As producer Mary Blakeman told the *Sentinel,* "Vida could hardly make a sound off-stage and spent the whole day desperately gargling. She was marvellous. Although she sounded rather husky, I could hear every word at the back of the theatre."

In 1980 it looked as though the same thing was going to happen again. *Wait Until Dark* was originally scheduled to run from 14th to 19th April with Maggie Brady playing the part of the blind woman, Susy Henderson. Maggie was taken ill and had to withdraw but Ann McArdle agreed to take over the part. There was, however, a complication. Ann was committed to the North Staffs Amateur Operatic Society's production of *The Music Man* at the Queen's Theatre in Burslem only a couple of weeks before our scheduled dates at the Mitchell. Fortunately we were able to put our production back by a week to give Ann more time to get to get to grips with the part which, of course, she did brilliantly in what the *Sentinel* reviewer Richard Howells described as "a rewardingly carefully studied performance".

The twice a year pattern was changed in 1981 because of our need to raise £10,000 to repair and restore our workshop in Hartshill. We were able to get an extra booking at the theatre in August and we took advantage of it to stage *How The Other Half Loves*.

Two years later it was another story. The play chosen for spring 1983 was *The Secret Tent* by Elizabeth Addyman, but for some reason we experienced in casting extreme difficulties the play and a full backstage crew was not available. Various options were explored but came to nothing. In the end the production was abandoned and, in the event, *The Secret Tent* was not staged until April 1985.

In 1993 we again put on three plays. From 1961 to 1992 it was our practice to present an evening of one-act plays in the summer. However around the end of that period we were approached by a local writer, Richard Griffiths, who asked us if we would be prepared to put on a new play he had written called *A Novel Inclination*. Richard, who lived in Wolstanton, was employed by Staffordshire County Council Music Service as a peripatetic clarinet teacher. Up to that time his links with the theatre had been through his music, as he was often to be found in the orchestra pit playing for local amateur operatic shows.

Richard's fascination with the theatre began after seeing Harold Pinter's *The Birthday Party* in the 60s, and from then on he had a vague but persistent desire to write plays. After one or two abortive attempts, including a rather gloomy TV play for a *Radio Times* competition, he decided to try his hand at comedy. The result was *A Novel Inclination*. Uncertain as to its strength as a viable play he sought a second opinion and, having supported Newcastle Players for some time and knowing several members personally, he asked us to read it. In fact we did better than just read it. We put it on as a play reading for our own entertainment and the guffaws that ensued from the assembled company assured Richard that, although the play needed refining, he was on the right track. Furthermore, to his delight, Ann McArdle said that, if they worked together on the refinements, she would be prepared to produce it some time in the future, which she did in July 1993.

"A Novel Inclination": (from left to right) Jim Ward, Jennifer Mallinson, Humphrey Gawthrop and Aline Lewis.

The Mitchell Full-Length Plays:

'Allo 'Allo
by Jeremy Lloyd & David Croft

A Friend Indeed
by William Douglas Home

A Letter from the General
by Maurice McLoughlin

A Novel Inclination
by Richard Griffiths

A Party to Murder
by Marcia Kash & Douglas E Hughes

All for Mary
by Harold Brooke & Kay Bannerman

An Inspector Calls
by J. B. Priestley

Because of the Lockwoods
by Constance Cox

Bedroom Farce
by Alan Ayckbourn

Beyond Reasonable Doubt
by Jeffrey Archer

Black Chiffon
by Lesley Storm

Bonaventure
by Charlotte Hastings

John Talbot (left) with Richard Stevens in a scene from "Hobson's Choice".

Breath of Spring
by Peter Coke

Celebration
by Keith Waterhouse & Willis Hall

Crown Matrimonial
by Royce Ryton

Dead Man's Hand
by Seymour Matthews

Dead Ringer
by Charles Ross

Deadly Nightcap
by Francis Durbridge

Dear Charles
by Alan Melville

Don't Listen Ladies
by Sacha Guitry

Don't Misunderstand Me
by Patrick Cargill

Double Cut
by Alfred Shaughnessy

Everybody Loves Opal
by John Patrick

Funny Money
by Ray Cooney

Good Night Mrs Puffin
by Arthur Lovegrove

Hobson's Choice
by Harold Brighouse

"Key for Two": (from left to right) Ann McArdle, Humphrey Gawthrop, Bruce Haycock, Caroline Heinsohn and Bob West.

How the Other Half Loves
by Alan Ayckbourn

It Runs in the Family
by Ray Cooney

Job for the Boy
by Dennis Driscoll

Key For Two
by John Chapman
(with Dave Freeman)

Ladies in Retirement
by Edward Percy
& Reginald Denham

Laura
by Vera Caspary & George Sklar

Lloyd George Knew My Father
by William Douglas Home

Look, No Hans!
by John Chapman
& Michael Pertwee

Love by Appointment
by Anthony Lesser

Man for the Job
by Dennis Driscoll

Midsummer Mink
by Peter Coke

Move Over Mrs Markham
by Ray Cooney & John Chapman

"Not Now Darling" (1998): (from left to right) Ian Wilson, Helen Foy and Sue Aynsley.

Murder in Mind by Terence Feely	*Outside Edge* by Richard Harris
My Giddy Aunt by Ray Cooney & John Chapman	*Party Piece* by Richard Harris
My Three Angels by Sam & Bella Spewack	*Portrait of Murder* by Robert Bloomfield
Nightmare by Norman Robbins	*Relative Values* by Noël Coward
Not in the Book by Arthur Watkyn	*Roar like a Dove* by Lesley Storm
Not Now Darling by Ray Cooney & John Chapman	*Sailor, Beware* by Philip King & Falkland Cary
Out of Focus by Peter Gordon	*Sand Castles* by Bob Larbey

"The Ghost Train" (2005): (from left to right) Richard Slater, Alan Hodgkinson, John Hough and Mike Egan.

School for Spinsters
by Roland Pertwee

Shadow in the Sun
by Maurice McLoughlin

She's Done It Again
by Michael Pertwee

Someone Waiting
by Emlyn Williams

Something to Hide
by Leslie Sands

Spring at Marino
by Constance Cox

Straight and Narrow
by Jimmie Chinn

Suddenly at Home
by Francis Durbridge

Suspect
by Edward Percy & Reginald Denham

Table Manners
by Alan Ayckbourn

Take Away the Lady
by Jimmie Chinn

The Amorous Prawn
by Anthony Kimmins

The Big Killing
by Philip Mackie

The Cure For Love
by Walter Greenwood

Jonathan Fernyhough and Ann McArdle in a scene from "The Heiress".

The Exorcism
by Don Taylor

The Ghost Train
by Arnold Ridley

The Heiress
by Ruth & Augustus Goetz

The House by the Lake
by Hugh Mills

The Importance of Being Earnest
by Oscar Wilde

The Irregular Verb To Love
by Hugh & Margaret Williams

The Late Edwina Black
by William Dinner & William Morum

The Rape of the Belt
by Benn W. Levy

The Secret Tent
by Elizabeth Addyman

The Secretary Bird
by William Douglas Home

The Shop at Sly Corner
by Edward Percy

The Strange Case of Blondie White
by Bernard Merivale & Jeffrey Dell

There Goes the Bride
by Ray Cooney & John Chapman

Therese
by Thomas Job

"When We Are Married": (from left to right) Aline Lewis, Dorothy Beardmore and Elizabeth Rowley.

Time and Time Again
by Alan Ayckbourn

Touch of Purple
by Elleston Trevor

Trap for a Lonely Man
by Robert Thomas

Two Dozen Red Roses
by Kenneth Horne

Two Into One
by Ray Cooney

Uproar in the House
by Anthony Marriott & Alistair Foot

Wait Until Dark
by Frederick Knott

When We Are Married
by J. B. Priestley

Who Killed Santa Claus
by Terence Feely

Witness for the Prosecution
by Agatha Christie

You Can't Take It With You
by Moss Hart & George S. Kaufmann

An Invitation

THE NEWCASTLE PLAYERS

request the pleasure of your company for the performance of three one-act plays Tickets, obtainable through your usual member, will be allocated on a first come first served basis.   Early booking is advised.   No admission charge

The plays being presented are :

HOUSE IN FERN ROAD
by Maud Cassidy & Peter Coke

The cast includes :

Richards Stevens, Joyce Pepper, Carol Adams, Hilary Baggaley,
Roderic Owens, Patricia Rowley

Produced by MICHAEL OWENS

APRIL DAWN
by Philip Johnson

The cast includes

Diane West, Sheelagh Kerry, Marilyn Hughes,
Robert West, Brian Hall, Dorothy Peasegood

Produced by JOHN TALBOT

DANGER ON THE RIGHT
by L. Du Garde Peach

The cast includes

Helena Meitz, Marjorie Griffiths, Paula Shaw.
Yvonne Harden, Ian Hillier-Brook

Produced by DENIS CONNELLY

Mitchell Memorial Youth Centre Theatre   .   .   Hanley

Saturday . September 25th . 1965   7.30 p.m.

Bayley Godwin Ltd. Newcastle

5. One-Act Plays and Other Performances

As recorded on pages 31 and 32 the first one-act play we presented was *The Bride* by Gertrude Jennings on Thursday, 26th July 1945. It was not, however, a public performance. Public performances of one-act plays had to wait another sixteen years.

The idea of staging one-act plays as a way of ascertaining the abilities of new producers, stage managers and actors was first mooted in 1958 and the plan was to incorporate two one-act plays in a Christmas party to which "a limited number of friends who are regular patrons" would be invited. The Executive Committee agreed to book the Priory Hall for Tuesday 16th December at a cost of £4.6.0. The arrangements for refreshments were to be the responsibility of the Social Committee.

Unfortunately the Priory Hall turned out to be fully booked so it was decided that we should approach the Mitchell Memorial Theatre for two nights between 18th January and 7th February and to enquire whether there was any special concession on the charge since it would be a private showing to members only without charge. This was not possible either so the idea was dropped.

The idea of one-act plays "primarily to develop the new and younger members" came up again at the March 1961 Executive Committee Meeting when it was agreed that Pat Mason would approach the Play Reading Committee with a view to selecting two one-act plays for presentation at the Mitchell Memorial Theatre.

This time things went more smoothly. Two plays were chosen (*Everlasting Flowers* and *Sunday Tea*), all the new members were used and the plays were presented at the Mitchell Memorial Theatre on Saturday, 15th July 1961. Admission was free as were the programmes but to defray expenses a silver collection was taken. The programme contained the following explanation:

> In recent years the Newcastle Players have recruited a number of new members the majority of whom are taking part in the two one-act plays presented tonight.

> The complete production is in the form of an experiment as a result of discussions and deliberations of our Production and Play Reading Committees.
> We sincerely hope you enjoy these performances and in thanking you for your patronage we look forward to seeing you with us at our future productions when these newcomers to the Players will take their place amongst our more experienced members.

At the following month's Executive Committee meeting Pat Mason suggested a similar operation the following year. This was approved after it was stated that the first evening of one-act plays had cost £43 less the silver collection of £27. Pat Mason was, however, requested to watch any excessive expenditure by way of costumes, etc.

The one-act play evenings ran from 1961 to 1992 and during that time nearly every new acting member of the Newcastle Players first appeared in a one-act play before taking to the stage in a major production.

The evenings of one-act plays had no special title to start with, but from 1967 we billed them as *AN EVENING OF ONE ACT PLAYS*. In 1982 this changed to *AN EVENING'S ENTERTAINMENT* with the addition of:

DIVERTISSEMENT
A musical interlude
by Ann McArdle, Geoff Price and Jim Ward
with Dorothy Leigh (piano)
compiled and introduced by Jim Ward

Then in 1985 the title became *A SUMMER EVENING'S ENTERTAINMENT*. There was no 'divertissement' but there were three plays. The final change came in 1989 with *PLAYS FOR A SUMMER EVENING*.

Some of the plays proved popular enough to repeat: *Sunday Tea* (1961 and 1970), *Dark Brown* (1964 and 1987), *The Faithful Widow of Ephesus* (1966 and 1976), *The Thistle in Donkey Field* (1967 and 1977), *Careful Rapture* (1968 and 1980) and *The Copper Kettle* (1974 and 1985).

By far the most popular author was Philip Johnson who wrote *Everlasting Flowers* (1961), *Dark Brown* (1964 and 1987), *Heaven on Earth* (1964), *April Dawn* (1965), *Green for Danger* (1980), *Master Dudley* (1982) and *World Without Men* (1985). This is perhaps not surprising since Doollee.com, the online database of playwrights and theatre plays, records that at one time the

Samuel French catalogue of published plays contained over fifty of Philip Johnson's one-act plays – more than any other author.

The complete list of one-act plays we performed between 1961 and 1992 is as follows:

A Family Affair
by Pamela Sykes

Family Voices
by Harold Pinter

A Family Occasion
by Jill Glew & A. C. Thomas

Fumed Oak
by Noël Coward

A Fishy Business
by Margaret Wood

Green for Danger
by Philip Johnson

A Lady in a Cage
by P. S. Laughlin

Harlequinade
by Terence Rattigan

Afternoon at the Seaside
by Agatha Christie

Heaven on Earth
by Philip Johnson

April Dawn
by Philip Johnson

Henry Hereafter
by Hal D. Stewart

At the Changing of the Year
by Malcolm Young

Home is the Hunted
by R. F. Delderfield

Careful Rapture
by Jack Popplewell

House in Fern Road
by Maud Cassidy & Peter Coke

Danger on the Right
by L. du Garde Peach

I Spy
by John Mortimer

Dark Brown
by Philip Johnson

In Black and White
by Sydney Box

Escape Route
by Stuart Ready

Keep Calm
by Louis Goodrich

Everlasting Flowers
by Philip Johnson

Knightsbridge
by John Mortimer

Life of Hercules: Page One
by Thomas Cruden

Master Dudley
by Philip Johnson

Murder Play
by Brian J. Burton

November Echo
by Pamela Sykes

One Hour to Dusk
by Anthony Booth

Pastiche
by Nick Hall

*Plaza Suite
(Visitor from Forest Hills)*
by Neil Simon

*Plaza Suite
(Visitor from Mamaroneck)*
by Neil Simon

Pop Goes the Patient
by Leonard Barnet

Queer Street
by John Donald Kelly

Rise and Shine
by Elda Cadogan

See If I Care
by Cherry Vooght

Some Are Born
by Nita Dawson

St. Simeon Stylites
by F. Sladen-Smith

Sunday Tea
by Terence Bowen

The Balwhinnie Bomb
by Gordon Daviot

The Bathroom Door
by Gertrude E. Jennings

The Copper Kettle
by Margaret Wood

The Editor Regrets
by Michael Brett

The Faithful Widow of Ephesus
by Thomas Cruden

The Gentle Rain
by Anthony Booth

The Invisible Worm
by Elda Cadogan

The Leopard
by Adrian Alington

The Lullaby
by Michael Dines

The Man in the Lane
by Tom & Mary Neild

The Monkey's Paw
by W. W. Jacobs
(dram. L. N. Parker)

The Patient
by Agatha Christie

The Playgoers
by Arthur Pinero

The Play-Reading
by Joan Honey

The Plot Thickens
by Mark Langham

The Rats
by Agatha Christie

The Sword is Double Edged
by Arthur Swinson

The Thistle in Donkey Field
by Richard Tydeman

There's Always Spring
by Arthur Lovegrove

This Desirable Cottage
by Anthony Booth

Wedding Breakfast
by William Dinner & William Morum

When The Bough Breaks
by Gwyn Clark

While the Circus Passes
by Isobel Lowman

World Without Men
by Philip Johnson

The one-act plays were generally staged at the Mitch, but in 1967 we were invited to repeat our performance of Saturday 23rd September on the following Monday evening for a student-only audience in the 320-seater Concourse in the College of Building at Shelton. The three plays were *The Leopard*, *The Thistle in Donkey Field* and *This Desirable Cottage*.

By the time our evenings of one-act plays came to an end – because of a lack at the time of new members to try out – the run had extended to three nights and the staging, which had originally been very simple, had gradually got more and more elaborate. Otherwise, we feared, our paying patrons would draw adverse comparisons with our full-length play productions.

In 1995 we were approached by the North Staffordshire branch of The Royal British Legion which was holding a Festival of Remembrance at The Kings Hall in Stoke on Saturday 11th November. It was to be the first Festival of Remembrance to be held in North Staffordshire since 1956. It was also the night before the dress rehearsal for our production of *An Inspector Calls* at the Mitchell. The Legion wrote to ask if we were prepared to take part, adding: "What we had in mind was a short 15 minute sketch, probably similar to either a 'DADS ARMY' or 'It ain't arfot', the script being totally in your hands."

Easier said than done. However, after exploring various avenues, we located two short sketches by Eric Ball of The Rep who was delighted to let us use them. So Eric's *The Beginning* and *Letters to Loved Ones* were performed on the night by Moira Hammond, Ann Hurlstone, Aline Lewis, Pat Mason, Val Owens, Geoff Price, Bob West and Di West, none of whom were involved directly in *An Inspector Calls*. But Ann McArdle (producer), John Hough (stage manager) and Chris Hammond (sound effects) certainly were.

It was a great success in spite of practical problems such as inadequate backstage facilities and chaotic dress rehearsal conditions. On the other hand the lighting and electrical technicians did us proud even though they were working under similar difficulties to ourselves. In all fairness, the Legion officials were probably blissfully ignorant of these problems. They expressed their appreciation publicly (in a letter to *The Sentinel*), privately (in a letter to our Secretary) and tangibly (in the form of a £25 donation to our funds).

It was an interesting example of cooperation between Newcastle Players, The British Legion and The Rep.

Another interesting cooperation with The Rep took place more recently. In 1994, Newcastle Players donated £1,000 to The Rep's new theatre building fund. Appropriate acknowledgements were made at the time and in due course plaques were affixed to seats K1 and K2 in the theatre recording for posterity our contribution to the new building. But in 2006, when we were seeking funding for the restoration and repair of our workshop, The Rep offered us the free use of their theatre for a fund-raising show.

This was entitled *The Best of Summertime* and took place on Saturday 9th September 2006. It comprised a one-act play (*A Small Affair* by Bob Larbey) in the first half and, after the interval, a *Musical Extravaganza* assembled and directed by Andrew Talbot, who had played Herr Otto Flick in our 2003 production of *'Allo 'Allo,* and featuring guest artistes as well as Newcastle Players members.

6. Authors, Producers and Directors

The Author

Although, as mentioned in the previous chapter, Philip Johnson was the most popular author of the one-act plays we produced, he is just pipped at the post overall by Ray Cooney and John Chapman who, between them wrote nine of the full-length plays we have presented.

The run started with *Not Now, Darling* by Cooney and Chapman which we presented first in 1979 and then repeated in 1998. The other Cooney/Chapman collaborations were *My Giddy Aunt* (1980), *Move Over Mrs Markham* (1986) and *There Goes the Bride* (1992). John Chapman wrote *Key For Two* (1988) with Dave Freeman and *Look, No Hans!* (1997) with Michael Pertwee. Finally *Two Into One* (1996), *Funny Money* (2000) and *It Runs in the Family* (2004) were solo efforts by Ray Cooney.

All these plays were farces and all were immensely successful. Yet prior to the first production of *Not Now, Darling* we had never done farce. A Ben Travers farce had been considered in the mid-thirties but it was rejected and farces continued to be rejected until late in the seventies. The main protagonist for this type of play at that time was John Talbot who, in fact, produced the 1979 version of *Not Now, Darling*, *Key For Two* and *Two Into One*. He also acted in *My Giddy Aunt* and *Move Over Mrs Markham*.

Generally speaking we do not have any direct contact with the authors of the plays we do. There have been exceptions though.

Arnold Ridley was the author of our very first production, *The Ghost Train* in 1935. It is not clear whether he actually came to see it then. Members of the Rowley family remember him visiting their house, although it seems more likely that that was in 1943 when a touring production of the play was on in Hanley. Whichever it was, he drew the sketch overleaf for Mary, John Rowley's eldest daughter. The dates at the top refer to our original production.

In 1987 Ben Devall, who later became our President, was made a Life Member of the society. At the time he was working on the backcloth for our production

> 17-19/1/35
> SMOKE
> With love from Amos Ridley

of *A Friend Indeed* by William Douglas Home, a fact which was mentioned in the reports of Ben's life membership in several local newspapers. This resulted in a rather unexpected but nevertheless very pleasant postscript, for Ben was delighted to receive a personal note written from his Hampshire home by William Douglas Home and this is reproduced here:

> Dear Mr Devall,
>
> I've got a press cutting telling me all about you.
>
> Good luck with your back-drop for 'A Friend Indeed' and please wish the cast good luck with the play.
>
> William Douglas Home

A few years later we did *Beyond Reasonable Doubt* by Jeffrey Archer and Jonathan Fernyhough, who was Public Relations Officer at the time, received the letter reproduced opposite from him.

The Producer or Director

What the author wrote has to be converted into what the audience sees and the person who is responsible for that and for running the rehearsals used to be called the producer. In the mid-fifties the professional theatre in England decided to follow the cinema practice and to adopt the title of director. We

> # Jeffrey Archer
>
> 22nd August 1994
>
> J Fernyhough Esq
> Newcastle Players
>
> Dear Mr Fernyhough,
>
> Many thanks for your letter of 8th August. May I take this opportunity of wishing the Newcastle Players every success with your new production of "Beyond Reasonable Doubt". I am only sorry that I shall not be in Newcastle during the week of 14th-19th November but look forward to hearing how it went.
>
> With best wishes.
>
> Yours sincerely
>
> Jeffrey Archer
>
> Alembic House 93 Albert Embankment London SE1 7TY 071 735 0077

were rather slow to change over in the Newcastle Players and the first time we referred to the director rather than the producer was in 2001.

From 1935 to 1944 all our plays were produced by John Rowley. Then *Ladies in Retirement* (1946) and *Winter Sunshine* (1947) were directed by John Rowley and produced by Mary Blakeman. There was just one more John Rowley production (*The Blue Goose*) in 1948 and that was followed by fifty-three Mary Blakeman productions over a period of nearly forty years. It was not an uninterrupted series however. During that that time there were five plays produced by Ray Backes, five by Paul Godfrey, one by Michael Owens,

The garage in Poolfield Avenue with its large upstairs room where so many rehearsals and other Newcastle Players events took place in the thirties and forties (see opposite page).

three by Alan Spriggs, one by Richard Stevens, six by John Talbot, one by Jim Ward and two by Bob West.

The last play produced by Mary Blakeman was *When We Are Married* in 1987. Since then plays have been produced (or directed as we now say) by Jonathan Fernyhough, Humphrey Gawthrop, Paul Godfrey, Ann McArdle, John Talbot and Jim Ward plus two guest directors, Ian W. Wilson and Pam Shufflebotham.

7. The Search for A Home of Our Own

When the Newcastle Players first came into existence in 1934, John Rowley and his family lived in a large house called "St Mary's" on the corner of Poolfield Avenue and Keele Road in Newcastle. His widowed mother lived on the opposite corner in a house then called "Roma" (it is now called "Deansgate House"). It had a large room over its garage (see picture opposite) which was used as, and referred to as, "the Newcastle Players' Rehearsal Room". Another name for it within the society was "The Den" and, although Mrs Rowley died in 1942, it was still used by the society as late as 1945, when the one-act play *The Bride* by Gertrude Jennings was presented there on 26 July of that year. "The Den" was a base, but it was not really a home of our own.

It is not clear from the society's records why we were without somewhere to perform in after our brief stay at Porthill. There are only references to the difficulties of having "no quarters". There was an investigation into the possible use of a church hall in School Street, Newcastle, but that came to nothing.

So, in 1945, the search for a home of our own began in earnest. The President, John Legge, was optimistic about the possibility of the society being able to obtain a lease on a disused chapel in Lower Street (pictured right). The book *Newcastle-under-Lyme 1173-1973,* which was commissioned by the borough to commemorate its octocentenary in 1973, says of this building : "Lower Street Chapel was built by the Wesleyans in 1799. They occupied it until 1861 when the Methodist Reform Church took it over until it was demolished in the early 1960s." It was in fact demolished to make way for the ring road and the site is now occupied by the Midway multi-storey car park.

In November 1946 we started our five-play run at the Parish Hall in Priory Road, but the search for a home of our own continued. Our plans – or aspirations – were revealed to our public when we moved to the Municipal Hall, Newcastle in October 1949. The programme for *Jupiter Laughs* – our first play there – contained this note:

> Some of our 'regulars' will, of course, recall the plays put on at Marsh St. Assembly Rooms before the war--since then we have, alas, been 'pushed around' but now we have embarked on a bigger venture by coming to this Theatre and we need your support so that our audiences will be large ones and in the fullness of time we shall be able to have our own little Theatre which in truth will be yours.

This was expanded upon eighteen months later when John Legge included the following paragraph in a foreword to the programme for *Bonaventure* (April 1951):

> We have been trying for some time now to get a place of our own. We offered to rent a building from the Corporation, the Society undertaking to do the necessary alterations, but the project fell through. We believe that there is a real, need in the Borough for a small intimate place where the local amateur societies would not be in competition with the professional companies.

What finally dashed our hopes for the Lower Street Chapel was a letter from the Town Clerk in December 1951 which stated that these premises were not available as they were still being used by the Housing Dept (not the Methodist Reform Church as mentioned above – GHP).

The search went on though. The idea of going outside Newcastle if suitable premises could be found was considered, but it was felt that we should remain in the Borough if possible and that we should spend another year looking for premises in Newcastle before we contemplated going further afield.

Various premises were suggested and investigated throughout 1952 and 1953. They included the former Salvation Army Barracks in Bath Street and a mill in Hempstalls Lane, both of which were found unsuitable for conversion to a theatre.

Two further possible buildings were the premises of Jones Moss & Co in Brunswick Street and Hanover Tile Fireplace Co in Hanover Street. A contemporary minute records that the Stage Manager and the Secretary "considered a very nice little theatre could be planned but we should require the Jones Moss premises and part of the Hanover Fireplace premises for a stage." The original price of the Jones Moss building was £10,000 but it was reported that they were prepared to accept offers and it might go down as low as £5500. Hanover were asking £3500 for their whole building and were not prepared at that time to sell part.

Towards the end of 1953 attention turned to the possible purchase of chapel premises in New Street, Wolstanton (since demolished and replaced by housing). This was debated at length at an Extraordinary General Meeting and finally rejected. One worry was that "We should be leaving Newcastle", but more importantly there was concern that buying the building would use up all our funds and the work involved in converting it while continuing to present our regular programme of plays would be too great a strain on our manpower resources.

However, it was decided that the Little Theatre Committee should "continue to function and continue to search for premises".

In 1955 the question of the Lower Street Chapel came up again and a letter was sent to the Town Council asking for reconsideration of our application for the use of the chapel as a theatre and pointing out that in Stoke-on-Trent there would be three privately owned amateur theatres whereas there would be none in Newcastle.

Enquiries were also made in 1956 about the possible use of Brunswick chapel as a theatre, but all of this came to nought and in August 1957 it was decided that, as the prospect of having our own theatre was becoming nothing more than a dream, the society's funds should be employed in procuring and running what was referred to as a clubroom.

Again various possibilities were explored and approaches were made to the Town Clerk and the Borough Surveyor, the latter providing information about several plots of land that were available in the borough. One which we expressed interest in was a site in Hassall Street used at the time as an open yard for storing cars. The Borough Surveyor said that there did not appear to be any objection in principle to us developing this and quotations were obtained for suitable buildings that could be erected on the land.

At this point the Newcastle Congregation of Jehovah's Witnesses became involved since they were interested in part of the Hassall Street site too. The

Borough Surveyor and the Area Planning Officer were of the opinion that in principle both organisations could be accommodated on the site but we would be expected to conform to certain restrictions regarding an acceptable fascia. By the end of 1958, however, we had come to the conclusion that the Hassall Street scheme was completely beyond our resources. The maximum that the committee felt that we should spend on such a project was £900, whereas the Hassall Street scheme would only give us one room and the whole site would cost over £1000.

Alternatives were considered in Shelton and Boundary Street, Newcastle but again came to nothing. While all this was going on ideas about the purpose of the building were changing. What had originally been thought of as a little theatre, then a clubroom eventually crystallised as somewhere to build and store scenery.

For the first twenty or so years of our existence we hired our sets. With mixed results. The *Sentinel* review of *The Ghost Train,* for example, commented on "scenery and effects much more elaborate than are normally attempted on the amateur stage". The set supplied for *Home at Seven*, however, was a disaster. The action of the play took place in the sitting room of a poorly-paid bank clerk's house in Kent. "The set that they sent," Eluned Mason recalled, "would have been absolutely ideal at Chatsworth. It was partly panelled, about a third of the way up, and right to the top of the set in blue and gold and green swirls with bunches of golden grapes. Can you imagine anybody having that sort of thing in an ordinary home?"

The only solution appeared to be to paint over all the fancy detail with Walpamur. Naturally the suppliers said that we had ruined a valuable set and several months of wrangling followed until agreement was reached on how much compensation we should pay.

That was in 1952, but it was not until 1959 that we decided to purchase a basic stock flats from Cresswells of Bury plus various other necessary fittings and to establish a scenery building section.

The original members who expressed a wish to join the section were Ray Backes, John Barstow, Bill Peake, Mary Blakeman, Ben Devall, Pat Mason, Monty Slater, Audrey Spriggs, Bill Stevens, John Talbot, Enid Tunstill and Peter Tunstill. New members were invited to join in the following note which appeared in the programme for our November 1959 play (*Witness for the Prosecution*) at the Mitchell Memorial Theatre:

SCENERY DESIGN

Some years ago it was customary for the Society to design and produce its own scenery for all its plays. However, as from the time we played in the Municipal Hall, Newcastle, we hired professional sets as the demands of the stage in that Hall were such that we had insufficient facilities to produce our own.

Now we have moved to this delightful theatre we have more room backstage and use of the workshops at the rear can be obtained for scenery design. In view of this improved position it is the intention of the Society to reorganise our scenery production section with a view to producing our own sets in time for the Autumn play next year.

We have a nucleus of members to start this section but we would like to recruit new members primarily for this purpose and in particular two Scenic Artists and two Stage Carpenters. We would be grateful if anyone interested in this work would apply for membership to the Secretary or any of our Officials.

As it happens our use of the Mitchell workshop never got off the ground. The authorities informed us that no general storage facilities were available in the workshop. We could keep scenery there while we were preparing it for a play but immediately after the play it would have to be removed. A solution was found in nearby Clough Street where Dorothy Wilson Dry Cleaning Ltd would rent us one of their ground floor warehouses at 12/6d a week inclusive of rates. We paid one year's rent in advance and moved in. That was in February 1960. It was originally for one year, but we stayed seven years even though conditions were hardly ideal. The space was so limited that, if somebody wanted to come in from the street while others were working on a flat supported on trestles, the flat had to be turned on its side to allow room for the door to open.

This problem was solved, if that is the right word, when the owners of the building announced that it was to be demolished to make way for developments in Clough Street. Towards the end of 1966 we found more spacious accommodation in a disused chapel at 18 West View, Wolstanton and we took up tenancy in February 1967 at an annual rent of £130 inclusive of rates. A working party was set up and during the summer of that year a number of very successful evenings took place when various members of the society showed great enthusiasm in painting and cleaning up the building.

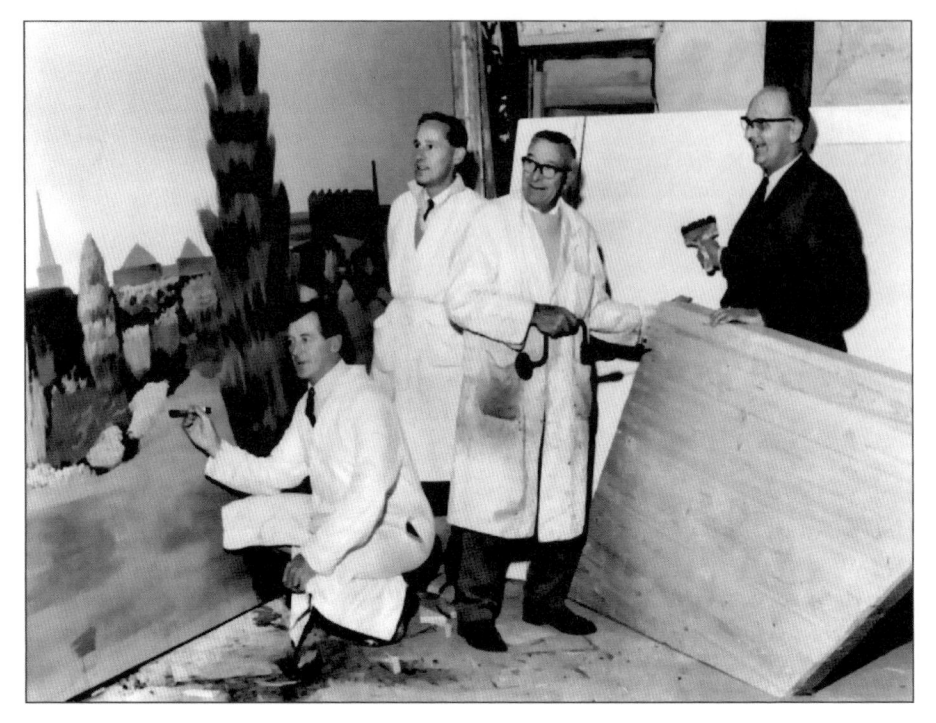

Arthur Gennery, Pat Mason, Bill Stevens and Peter Tunstill working on the set for "Dear Charles" at 18 West View in October 1968.

Things started to go sour the following year when Newcastle Borough Council informed us that the landlord, contrary to the terms of the lease, was refusing to pay the rates. We had to pay these as the occupiers of the premises but the landlord refused to negotiate any reduction in the rent. In May 1969 in view of the trouble where having at West View it was agreed that all members should look out for a new suitable scenery store. The President, John Barstow, had noticed that a hall at Hartshill appeared to be unused and decided to investigate.

How that turned out is the subject of the next chapter. The building we used at 18 West View has since been demolished and there is now a recently built private house there.

8. A Home of Our Own
The Newcastle Players Theatre Workshop

The property which John Barstow had noticed was a building in Hartshill Road, Hartshill – number 287 to be precise (pictured right). Driving in the direction of Stoke from Newcastle it is between Hartshill Church and the Tesco Express store and filling station but on the opposite side of the road. It was built in 1858 by the potter Colin Minton Campbell (whose initials are set in the brickwork over the front door) and it was originally known as Hartshill Working Men's Institution. Its purpose was to provide a reading room and recreation facilities for the Minton pottery factory employees living in the adjacent cottages which had been built some years earlier by Colin Minton Campbell's uncle Herbert Minton. The cottages are in fact known as the Minton Cottages and there is also a street behind the church called Minton Street.

More recently it had been used as a church hall and John Barstow had an emotional interest in the building since he and his wife Lulu had held their wedding reception there. John usually gave it a glance whenever he drove past it and he had noticed about the time that we were looking for premises that the church seemed to be no longer using it. In June 1969 he reported to the Executive Committee that the Church Commissioners were interested in selling the hall. He had looked at it and, although there were apparently a few parts of the roof which let in water, this was not considered serious. Having talked to the firm of solicitors handling the sale he understood that if we made an offer of £500 for this freehold property subject to all conditions it was likely that it would be accepted. The committee endorsed the proposal and decided that we should go ahead and buy it.

In November 1969 we formally took possession of the building which we renamed "Newcastle Players Theatre Workshop" and we started to deal with the necessary repair work which at that time was expected to cost £300.

When the institute was formally opened in January 1859 *The Staffordshire Sentinel and Midland Counties Advertiser* reported that this "beautiful building" was Gothic in style and consisted of a reading room, or lecture hall, 40ft. by 20ft. with a "permanent platform at the end opposite the entrance" and "a commodious residence for the hallkeeper adjoining". The latter was, of course, not included in the Newcastle Players purchase. "The main front of the reading room," the report continued, "is in brick, but highly relieved by white and grey stone, black brick, marble, wood, and black and red tiles, the whole of these varied materials being blended together in excellent harmony, and with artistic effect; and producing that picturesqeness which is evidently the chief quality aimed at in the exterior. The entrance to the hall is through a spacious arched doorway, the arch being supported by Purbeck marble columns, ornamented by carved Caen stone, the gable bearing the monogram of Mr. Campbell, in appropriate characters."

At some time in the past a kitchen and toilet were built on at the rear of the building. To make it more suitable for our purposes we have made a number of internal modifications such as removing the small stage referred to in the newspaper report and fitting a false ceiling to help retain heat at floor level. Extensive remedial action was also necessary in the early days against dry rot.

The floor area is large enough for our workshop team to erect the set for each production and work on it in the form that it will be on the stage at the Mitchell Memorial Theatre. At one time we also conducted rehearsals there too, but there were a number of disadvantages to that. For example, at the theatre the actual playing area usually extends several feet in front of the leading edge of the scenery, but the workshop floor is not wide enough for that. In addition the producer (or director as we now say), the prompter and other people found themselves with no alternative but to sit in the acting area, as can be seen in the photograph opposite taken during a rehearsal of *The Secret Tent* (April 1985). There was also the fact that, to hold a rehearsal in the set, the workshop team had to clear it of all their equipment and then get it out again the next time they we were working, which of course reduced the time that had available.

On the other hand we have on occasion used the workshop for things such as a jumble sale, social events and training sessions.

Rehearsing "The Secret Tent" at the workshop in 1985. In the picture are Bruce Haycock, Jim Ward, Vida Stevens, Ann McArdle and Paul Godfrey.

In the programme for A *Letter from the General* (November 1970) we included the following note:

Newcastle Players Theatre Workshop

We would like to take this opportunity to thank you for your loyal and continued support. Thanks to this support we have been able to acquire our own Theatre Workshop, where we can store scenery and construct the sets prior to bringing them to the Mitchell Memorial Youth Centre Theatre. This is a wonderful asset and we do thank you sincerely.

In 1977 the area surrounding and including the workshop was officially designated the Hartshill Conservation Area and we were informed by the City of Stoke-on-Trent's Director of Environmental Services that:

1. No part of any building within the Conservation Area shall be treated with any form of cement rendering or stone cladding including imitation stonework cladding without the prior consent of the Local Planning Authority.

2. No external brickwork of any building within the Conservation Area shall be painted without the prior consent of the Local Planning Authority.

The impact of the creation of the conservation area was brought home to us in April 1980 by the letter we received from the Director of Environmental Services reproduced opposite. This was the start of a period of intense activity aimed at renovating the workshop. Although the initial letter only referred to woodwork, further investigation revealed a wider range of problems.

A £10,000 appeal was launched and various fund-raising activities were initiated. These included:

- A Buy-a-Brick Campaign

- The presentation of an extra play in August 1981 (*How the Other Half Loves* by Alan Ayckbourn) for which some members cancelled holidays so that they could take part

- A sponsored cycle ride from Newcastle-on-Tyne to Newcastle-under-Lyme by Bruce Haycock supported by a team led by Philip Eardley

- A jumble sale, a coffee evening, a bring & buy sale, quiz, china sale, cheese and wine evening and so on.

By the time of our 1983 Annual Meeting the President, Bill Stevens, was able to report that the major part of the restoration work had been successfully completed. This had been possible due to grants from the City of Stoke-on-Trent and the Staffordshire Councils, the fund-raising efforts by the Players themselves, but above all, to the generosity of the Society's patrons, without whose help and support the project would have proved extremely difficult.

The Conservation Order on the building had created some considerable difficulties, he said, but these had been overcome and the standard of work had been praised by Mr John Shryane, the City's Director of Environmental Services. In a letter to the Society he not only congratulated the Newcastle Players on the success of the project but added, "The building has been carefully restored and is now a credit to the Hartshill Conservation area"!

Later that year two alterations to the interior of the building were considered, one we proceeded with and one we rejected.

City of Stoke-on-Trent

John Shryane, M.R.T.P.I., R.I.B.A., F.R.S.A.
Director of Environmental Services

Mr F A Tunstill
Blithe Cottage
Tavistock Crescent
NEWCASTLE
Staffordshire ST5 3NW

P.O. Box 207
Unity House
Hanley
Stoke-on-Trent ST1 4QL

Telephone Extn 2292
Stoke-on-Trent 29611 (STD Code 0782)

Your ref

Our ref PL/MGD/AJB (Mr M G Downs)

Date 25 April 1980

Dear Sir

Premises of The Newcastle Players,
287 Hartshill Road, Hartshill.

I understand that you are the Secretary of the Newcastle Players who occupy the above building.

This property, as you will be aware, lies within the Hartshill Conservation Area, which is a protected area under several pieces of environmental legislation.

It has recently been brought to my attention that the woodwork of 287 Hartshill Road is currently in a rather poor state of repair. My assistant has recently visited the site and is of the opinion that if the external woodwork of the property is not satisfactorily restored and repainted in the near future, then wood rot will become chronic and very expensive to remedy.

I would therefore urge you on behalf of the Newcastle Players to take the necessary action to preserve this building at an early stage, and thereby maintain the quality of the environment in the Conservation Area and avoid storing up more serious and costly problems for the future.

Yours faithfully

John Shryane

Director

20

The newspaper report of the official opening mentioned earlier described the interior in the following terms:

> Internally, the hall though simply furnished, is of striking appearance, being lofty, well proportioned, light, and possessing an air of great

> comfort . . . The roof is an open timbered one, and perhaps the most original and effective part of the design. A lantern, constructed in it, supplies the room with abundant and agreeable light, while a row of quatrefoils running round the top of the lantern carries off the vitiated air. This admirable arrangement, by the way, one too often neglected, must, we think, account for the comfortable feeling which those who have passed any time in the room have experienced.

Those who used the building in the nineteenth century were not used to central heating and must have been more tolerant of the cold in winter than we are now. A hundred or so years after the hall was opened we found the lofty design something of a drawback, since any heat generated at floor level rose into the lantern leaving the occupants shivering below. Our solution was to fit a suspended ceiling which may have cut out the "abundant and agreeable light" but certainly created a pleasanter atmosphere in the working area.

The other change considered was to modify the gallery at the entrance end so that it could be utilised for committee meetings. This was, and still is, accessed via a cast-iron spiral staircase. Its floor is not flat but stepped. The possibility of installing a single-level floor and closing off the gallery with glass partitioning was investigated. This would have created a room approximately 9 ft wide by 25 ft deep, but after careful consideration it was felt that it would take up space currently used for storage and a room that size with a possible twelve committee members would not be at all comfortable. It was agreed, therefore, to take no further action with this.

On 15th March 1993 the Department of National Heritage listed the Newcastle Players Theatre Workshop as a building of special architectural or historic interest, making it a Grade II Listed Building. The cottages on either side of the workshop and Hartshill Church are also listed buildings.

Grade II Listed Building status places even greater restrictions on what we can do with the building than those applicable to the conservation area. In a written reply to a parliamentary question in 1998 about what this entails the then Minister for the Arts, Alan Howarth MP (now Baron Howarth of Newport, said: "The Planning (Listed Buildings and Conservation Areas) Act 1990 requires the owner of any listed building to obtain listed building consent for any works of demolition or for any works of alteration or extension which would affect its character as a building of special architectural or historic interest. The carrying out of such works without prior consent is a criminal offence."

Over 180 buildings in The Potteries are listed. The Heritage Number of our workshop is 67a and details of it can be found at www.thepotteries.org in the section devoted to "Listed Buildings in Stoke-on-Trent". There are three photographs of our workshop plus the following description:

> 1859 red brick and stone dressing with plain tile roof, designed by George Gilbert Scott
> Institute financed by Colin Minton Campbell

In 1996 we started to examine the possibility of restoring the exterior of the building to its former glory and carrying out considerable refurbishment to the interior with a view to converting it into The Newcastle Players Theatre Centre, which would have involved extensive alterations both inside and out.

The exterior work was to involve cleaning, treating and, where possible, preserving the exterior fabric of the building, replacing the paved area at the front and reglazing the windows in keeping with their original 1850s style. The result would have been not only to enhance the appearance of our building but also to add to the appeal of the residential property on either side known as the Minton Cottages (on the left) and the Campbell Cottages (on the right).

Internally we intended to enlarge and enclose the existing balcony, insert a floor on a single level and create a new room which would serve as our headquarters, meeting room, social room and rehearsal room.

The kitchen and toilet facilities were to be transferred to the area at the front of the building under the new room, while the existing kitchen, paint store, toilet and the boiler room beneath were to be gutted and refurbished after the floor has been lowered to the same level as the rest of building to become our workshop, tool store and small effects room.

Last but not least the floor in the main hall was to be attended to. According to the professional advice we received, the flooring was in excellent condition and the quality of the timber probably superior to flooring which could be purchased today. However, after almost a century and a half of use, it had developed a slope from one side to the other which created (and still creates) some problems for our set builders. This we intended to correct.

We were planning to carry out this work between April and August 1997 under the supervision of the architect Anthony Blacklay of Nantwich, who had considerable experience in dealing with historical buildings.

It was, of course, going cost a considerable sum of money. To this end we submitted an application to the Arts Council of England for a grant from the National Lottery Fund. However, we were also required to provide what is known as "partnership funding". We, therefore, committed £5,000 from our own reserves as well as approaching a number of charitable trusts, the relevant local authorities and other bodies for assistance and also carrying out several special fund-raising activities with the aim of raising a further £5,000.

Preparing our Lottery bid took longer than hoped. We abandoned ideas of doing the work in 1997 and reset our sights on the summer of 1998. We were eventually in a position to submit our application in July 1997. Basically this was a twelve page form accompanied by a further fifty pages of supporting documentation. There then followed innumerable telephone calls and letters from the Arts Council requesting clarification of various points. At one stage the clarifying documentation supplied was three times bigger than the original application and weighed over a kilogram. At another stage we received a two-page letter with yet more questions and a request that our reply be in the hands of the Arts Council within five days. There were times, it must be admitted, when we felt that we had overcome one hurdle only to be faced by another.

We were encouraged by one letter which said that we had submitted a model application and requesting our permission to use it as an example to be followed by other applicants. In spite of this, though, in December 1997 we received the response to our application. It contained the crucial but disappointing sentence: "The Arts Council of England has decided not to approve a grant of National Lottery funding for this project."

This meant that, after a lot of work and the expenditure of several thousand pounds on architect's and other professional fees, we were no further forward. In fact we were worse off financially than when we started.

So where did we go wrong?

To obtain such funding it is necessary to satisfy eight criteria:

1. Benefit to the public (including access for disabled people)
2. Long-term effect on the organisation's financial stability
3. Amount of partnership funding
4. Quality of design and construction
5. Quality of artistic activities planned

6. Relevance to local, regional and national plans for the arts
7. Contribution of artists, craftspeople and film and video makers
8. Quality of the organisation's plans for education and marketing

We had been led to believe in our preliminary negotiations with West Midlands Arts that, in the event of an application been rejected, the reason for the rejection would be given. In the event all we were told initially was that the Arts Council felt our application "was less strong in respect of . . . the quality of design and construction".

Further discussions with West Midlands Arts eventually gave us to understand that our project had not been ambitious enough. We had attempted to keep the costs within a budget of £100,000, since this would have meant our only having to find ten per cent of the cost from our own or other resources. Reading between the lines of subsequent correspondence seemed to indicate that the Arts Council would have preferred us to go for a much bigger project, possibly costing £150,000 or even £200,000 and requiring us to find twenty-five per cent of the cost. In other words our contribution would have had to go up from £10,000 to possibly as much £50,000, which we believed to be beyond our resources or our ability to raise.

In view of this, plus the fact that the money available to the arts had been reduced and the number of applications had increased, we decided to abandon our plans to refurbish the workshop in a single stage with the help of National Lottery funding. Since then we have spent several thousand pounds on partial repairs to the roof but any further work will depend on the availability of funds.

As this is being written we are faced with the urgent need to carry out further repairs to the roof and to replace the floor. It is estimated that this will cost in the region of £15,000 and we do not have that amount of money in our reserves. A number of members have made a commitment to make regular financial contributions and various other fund-raising activities are being carried out.

In the meantime of course the workshop continues to be used for its main purpose – housing our stock of scenery and preparing the set for the next play.

9. . . . and Back to Marsh Street

Early minutes refer to meetings taking place in "the Rehearsal Room, Poolfield Avenue". This was in fact the large room over the garage at "Roma", the home of John Rowley's mother pictured on page 56. From 1941 meetings were also held in the Borough Arms, Westlands Tennis Pavilion, Ryecroft School, the Castle Hotel, members' homes and a variety of other venues in and around Newcastle.

One of these venues was Newcastle Guild Hall in the High Street. The 1950 Annual General Meeting was held there on Sunday, 2nd April but, as the minutes record, it was apparently not a pleasant experience:

> There were 28 members present and all registered either by the spoken or unspoken word their disapproval of the atmosphere in this august edifice. The Secretary offered his apologies for the absence of any heat in the building but explained it was a matter unfortunately beyond his control.

Fortunately a new venue had become available a few months earlier: Newcastle Arts Centre at Pitfield House in the Brampton. In fact by the time of that particular AGM we had already used it for the first time a couple of weeks earlier for a committee meeting and we were to stay there for a further forty-nine years.

We held our first meeting at the Pitfield House Arts Centre on Friday 10th March 1950 and our last on Thursday 18th March 1999. Mary Blakeman was present on both occasions, in 1950 as a member of the Executive Committee and in 1999 as a special guest of the committee.

We have lost count of how many times we used Pitfield's facilities over nearly half a century. Mary Blakeman alone is estimated to have conducted somewhere in the region of 900 rehearsals there, not to mention all the committee meetings, play readings and other events we used it for. Yet, when the council decided to close Pitfield House, the then leader of the Borough Council, writing to our secretary, described our usage dismissively as 'casual'. It is a fact that we had stopped using the Arts Centre for rehearsals some time earlier, since we had finally decided that, spacious as the rooms must have

Pitfield House in The Brampton, home of the Newcastle Arts Centre from 1949 to 1999.

seemed when the building was a private residence, they were much smaller than the stage at the Mitchell Memorial Theatre and adapting from one to the other could be a problem. We therefore sought and found alternatives for rehearsal purposes. These included the Seabridge Community Centre and various church halls including the Methodist Rooms in Merrial Street where we had staged our first sixteen productions in the thirties and forties.

But it was for our Executive Committee meetings that we returned permanently to the Marsh Street Rooms, as they were called in 1935, and all such meetings have been held there since 1999.

10. Anniversaries

There have been a number of important anniversaries in the history of the Newcastle Players but the first one we celebrated was a little premature.

Coming of Age?

The Executive Committee held a meeting on Sunday 26th September 1954, the main business of which was to discuss "A Social Function on the occasion of the 21st Anniversary of the Newcastle Players". It was proposed and agreed that the 21st Birthday Celebration should "take the form of a private party at a cost not exceeding £1 a head, the charge to members being 10/-, under 21 5/-, the deficit to be met out of the society's Subscription Fund. Non-member wives or husbands should be included as members for this purpose".

In a note in the programme for our "21st Anniversary" production of *His Excellency* two months later the then President, John Legge, referred to "the first night twenty-one years ago when the curtain went up on *The Ghost Train*". It was actually 19 years, 9 months and 3 weeks. Obviously nobody had checked the date.

Programmes and other items printed in 1935 and 1936 stated "Founded 1934". Yet later on the society started to claim that it had been founded in 1933. It was not until 1975, when we celebrated our 40th anniversary, that we stopped quoting the earlier date on our letterhead, although the programme for *Trap For A Lonely Man* (November 1973) stated that "The first production of the Newcastle Players was *The Ghost Train* by Arnold Ridley, presented at the Marsh Street Rooms, Newcastle on 17th, 18th and 19th January, 1935".

There may be a clue to the earlier date in a *City Times* feature on the society dated 9th March 1960 which says that the society was "tentatively formed in 1933". However, for many years now we have acknowledged 1934 as the year the society was founded with our first production in January of the following year.

So the 21st Birthday Party was held on 10th January 1955 and the minutes of the February 1955 Executive Committee contain the following description:

John Legge (President) cuts the 21st Birthday cake watched by (left to right) Phyllis Showan, John Barstow (Vice-President), Mac Showan (Secretary), Hedley Strachan (Treasurer) and Win Strachan.

The evening in question was a dinner at Clayton Lodge Hotel to celebrate the coming of age of the Players. The President, Mr. J. Legge, was in the chair and many of the old Newcastle Players were present. An excellent dinner was served and after the speech "of the Newcastle Players had been moved by Mr. Connelly" (sic), the large birthday cake was cut. Telegrams were received from many old players and friends and each member received a plaque designed and produced at the works of one of our members, Mr J. Steventon, with the member's name on the back. A photograph was taken. Altogether a most enjoyable evening was held and appreciation was expressed by many members.

Silver Jubilee

The Silver Jubilee followed closely on the heels of the 21st Birthday party.

The ballroom at the Grand Hotel in Hanley was booked for the evening of Thursday, 25th September 1958 together with "a three-piece orchestra" and seven-course dinner. The cost would be slightly over £1 per head. The Executive Committee apparently agreed to cover the cost from the society's funds up to £1 per head and the Social Committee said that if the Executive Committee allocation of £1 per head was final, then any excess could be taken from the Social Committee funds. There is no record of what the final outcome was.

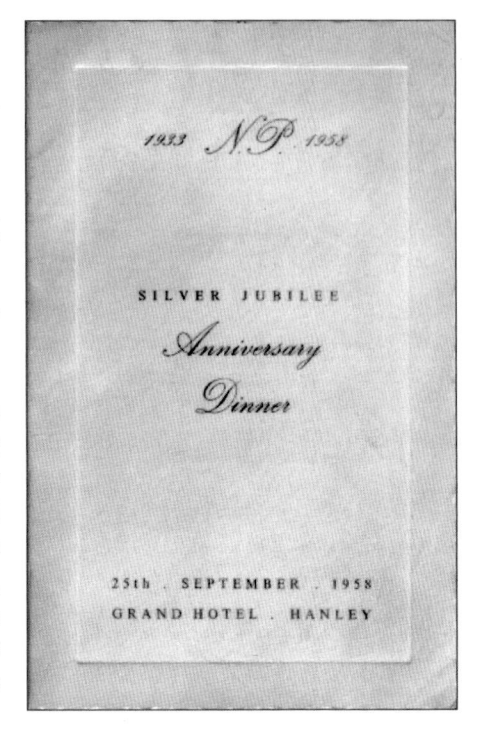

The menu for the Silver Jubilee Anniversary Dinner was:

HORS D'ŒUVRES

CONSOMMÉ BRUNOISE

SUPREME OF TURBOT NORMANDE

ROAST SURREY CHICKEN WITH BACON ROLLS
POTATO CROQUETTES
BUTTERED GARDEN PEAS
BRUSSELS SPROUTS

COUPE SINGAPORE

CHEESES VARIOUS, BISCUITS

COFFEE

Pictures of the Silver Jubilee event, one of which is reproduced above, appeared in the following night's "Evening Sentinel" and "The Staffordshire Weekly Sentinel" of Friday, 3rd October 1958. Seven of the eight people sitting on the floor at the front are (from left to right) Janet Mason, John Talbot, Joy West, Ann Barstow, Margaret Copeland, Yvonne Harden and Marie Backes. We have been unable to identify the eighth. Seated on the row behind are Eluned Mason, Lulu Barstow, Peter Tunstill, John Legge, John Barstow, Hedley Strachan, Mary Blakeman and Celia Connelly.

40th Anniversary

The 30th Anniversary slipped by, apparently unnoticed, but anniversary celebrations returned with a bang in 1975 with a 40th Anniversary Celebration Party at The Old Vicarage in Hanford (see invitation and photograph on the next page).

Not only were photographs taken but the proceedings were recorded on tape and are now held in the Newcastle Players' sound archives. John Barstow proposed the toast of The Newcastle Players and Enid Tunstill replied on behalf of the society. There was also a ditty written and performed by Enid Tunstill and Bob West. All three throw light on the society's first forty years and the society as it was in 1975. The ditty can be found in the next chapter and John's and Enid's speeches are reproduced in Appendix B at the end of the book.

The 40th Anniversary group photograph: The three sitting on the floor at the front are (from left to right) Kath Walsh (who became Kath O'Donnell later in the year), Philip Eardley and Susie Thomas. Behind them are Joan Osborne (née Connelly), Bill Stevens, Lulu and John Barstow, Jo Rowley, Peter Tunstill, Eluned Mason, and (with balloon) Pat Mason.

| 1935 | NEWCASTLE PLAYERS | 1975 |

40th Anniversary Celebration Party

The President and Executive Committee
request the pleasure of the company of

Mr & Mrs Peter Tunstill

as members of the Newcastle Players
on Friday, January 17th, 1975, at 8.00 p.m.
at The Old Vicarage, Hanford

Dress Informal

R.S.V.P. to J. F. Barstow, Esq., Edge Cottage, Endon

The 50th Anniversary group photograph: Seated on the floor at the front are (from left to right) Joan Crew, Di West, Paul Godfrey, June Godfrey, Bob West, Mick Whewell, Val Owens, Judith Whewell and Joy Jackson. Behind them are Ceilia Connelly, Ben Devall, Jo Rowley, Eluned Mason, Bill Stevens, John Talbot, Ann Hurlstone, Peter Tunstill, Joan Osborne and Mary Blakeman. The author is kneeling on the left between the two front rows.

There are more Golden Jubilee photographs on the next page.

Golden Jubilee

1984, our Golden Jubilee year, was marked with a party at the Wheatsheaf Inn at Onneley (photograph above) and productions of *The Cure for Love* and *Outside Edge*. The latter was notable for a couple of innovations.

One of the things we did to mark the special occasion was to publish our first ever magazine-style programme and the only one we've ever done in A4 format, but this is dealt with in more detail in the chapter about programmes.

The other innovation led indirectly to our talk called *A Word On Plays* which too is the subject of another chapter.

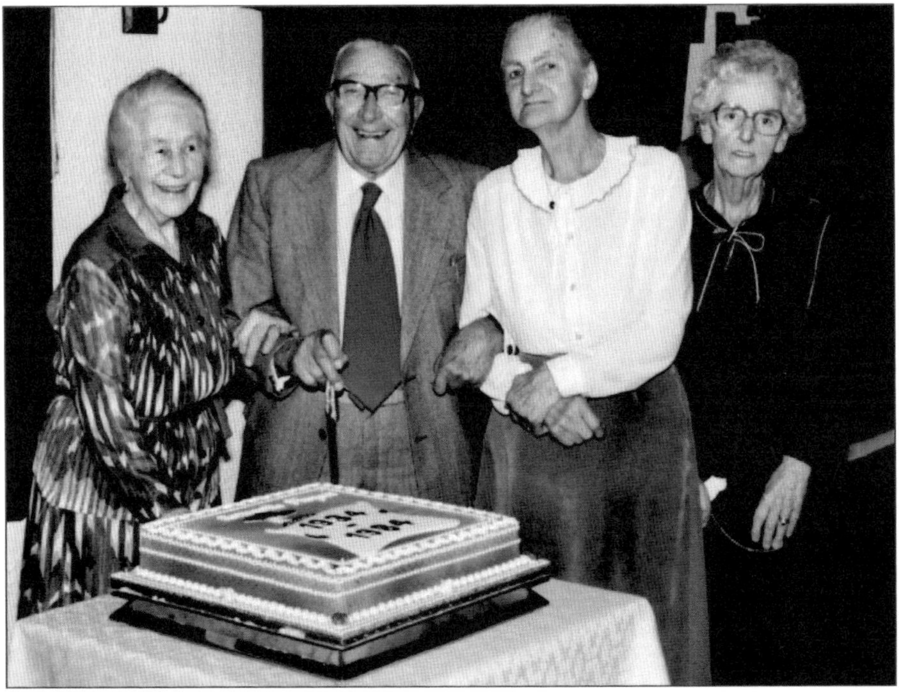

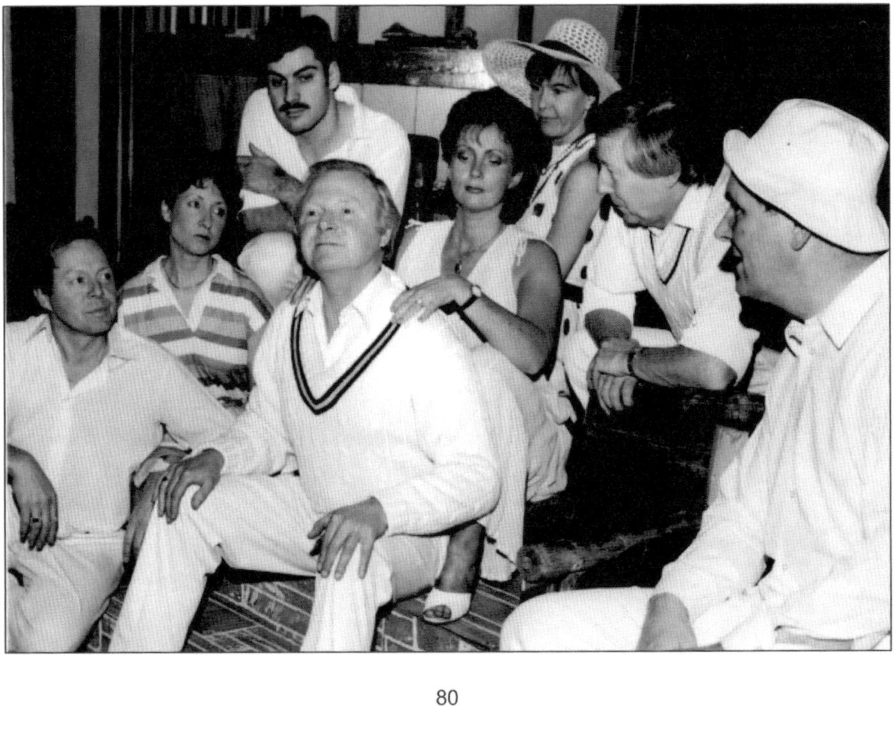

60th Anniversary

1994, our 60th Anniversary year, got under way in January with a Fancy Dress Party at Bob and Di West's house in Church Lawton. Other social events over the next twelve months included an Italian Evening at Ray Gennery's house in Baddeley Green, a couple of barbecues, a country walk at Dimmingsdale near to Alton, a dinner-dance at the North Stafford Hotel in Stoke and a Christmas Lunch at the Clayton Lodge Hotel in Newcastle.

We had intended to do a full-length play in the summer, as we had done with *A Novel Inclination* the previous year. Unfortunately this plan had to be abandoned, as there were not enough acting members available.

Our 60th Anniversary Production was *Beyond Reasonable Doubt* by Jeffrey produced by John Talbot. Following the shortage of actors in the summer it was good to see a cast of fourteen take the stage in November in what John Fox, reviewing the play for the Evening Sentinel, described as "a worthy celebration of Newcastle Players' high standards in amateur drama".

Although not specifically designed as part of our 60th Anniversary celebrations, one event which took place during the year deserves mention. That was our £1000 donation to the appeal launched by Stoke-on-Trent Repertory Theatre, or The Rep, to enable that society to move from the cramped conditions in its old theatre to new purpose-built premises in Leek Road.

The actual presentation took the form of a small ceremony held in our workshop on Tuesday, 20th September 1994 to hand over our donation. The cheque was presented to Ken Lowe and Richard Masters of The Rep by our President, Ben Devall, and Treasurer, Pat Mason. Ken referred to our gift as "not only generous but gracious" and he told us that, when the Rep's members were told about it at their AGM, there was an audible gasp followed by spontaneous applause.

Golden Jubilee photographs opposite:

Top: Bill Stevens prepares to cut the Golden Jubilee cake. Also in the photograph are Eluned Mason, Jo Rowley and Joan Osborne.

Bottom: The cast of the 1984 production of "Outside Edge"; (from left to right) Bob West, Janet Banks, John Turner, John Talbot, Sue Aynsley, Prue Winnett, Geoff Price and Jim Ward.

The photograph above shows The Rep's Ken Lowe and Richard Masters receiving our cheque from Newcastle Players President Ben Devall and Treasurer Pat Mason on the set (far from complete at that stage) of "Beyond Reasonable Doubt" in our theatre workshop in Hartshill.

For the benefit of the photographers we borrowed a giant presentation cheque (see photograph above) from the Midland Bank and had it suitably printed with the amount (£1000) and the names of the recipient and donor. A couple of days before the ceremony John Fox gave us a very favourable mention in his *Prompt Corner* column in the *Evening Sentinel*. He wrote:

> Certainly one society that believes in community spirit is Newcastle Players, who have donated £1,000 towards Stoke Rep's new theatre building fund. An impossible action for most amateur companies of course, but the Players' magnificent gesture sets an example of supporting others that could be followed by everyone interested in amateur drama, even in small ways.

70th Anniversary

And now we have celebrated our 70th Anniversary with our 2004/2005 season. It started off with a lunch party at Slater's Country Inn, Baldwins Gate on Sunday, 22nd August 2004 and was brought to a close by a similar event at The Wilbraham Arms, Alsager on Saturday, 23rd April 2005. Between the two we staged *It Runs in the Family* in November 2004 and a revival of our very first production, *The Ghost Train,* in April 2005. The icing on the cake was that it was the first season we had been eligible to enter the Mitchell Memorial Theatre's Full Length Play Festival and we finished up winning four of the eight awards we were eligible for. Again that is discussed in more detail in another chapter.

The lunch in Baldwins Gate was attended by Joan Osborne, our longest serving member, and two other very long-serving members, Vida Stevens and Enid Frieder. Our current President, Buffie Rowley, took a nostalgic look back over our first seventy years. As always, Buffie was at pains to point out that she wasn't actually there when the society was founded, but she might at the time have been a thought her parents' minds. That is if they weren't too preoccupied with getting the new society off the ground, for her father John, backed by her mother Josephine, was one of the driving forces – if not the driving force – that got the Newcastle Players started in 1934.

Our first production was *The Ghost Train* by Arnold Ridley, who later became known to television audiences as Mr Godfrey in *Dad's Army*. We staged the play in Newcastle for three nights in January 1935 and Buffie understood that Arnold Ridley actually came to see the production, although, as is explained in Chapter 6, it was probably a few years later that he visited the Rowley family. One thing that is certain is that the prompter on that occasion was the 17 year old Joan Connelly, later Joan Osborne.

Buffie mentioned many other members who had served the society over the years and were now remembered with great respect and affection. In particular she mentioned three who were present at the lunch, namely Pat Mason, Vida Stevens and Enid Frieder.

Vida made her debut with the society in April 1939, when she played Sylvia Armitage in *Murder on the Second Floor*. Enid, then Enid Durrant, followed a couple of years later in November 1941 playing Margery Harvey in *Dear Octopus* with Vida in the part of Laurel Randolph. Since then they both appeared on stage and backstage in too many plays to mention, backed up for

Around fifty members and friends of the Newcastle Players gathered at Slater's Country Inn in Baldwins Gate on Sunday, 22nd August 2004 for a celebratory lunch to kick off our Seventieth Anniversary year. We were delighted that Joan Osborne (extreme right of the front row in the section of the group photograph above), our longest serving member, was able to be present, as were two other very long serving members, Vida Stevens and Enid Frieder (extreme left of the front row in the section of the group photograph on the opposite page).

many years off-stage and front-of-house by their husbands Bill Stevens and Peter Tunstill.

Pat Mason's parents, like Buffie's, were involved in the society from the very beginning, although Pat's mother, Eluned, was not allowed to become a member until some time later when the rules were amended to allow non-Catholics to join. Pat himself made his acting debut as a small boy in the society's third production, *Quality Street* in 1936, long before he was old enough to become an actual member.

11. Ditties

Over the years ditties have become an important part of the Newcastle Players ethos. These days hardly an after-play party goes by without some aspiring poet laureate reciting a poetic account of the latest production. Regrettably some have not survived but others have been recorded in our bulletin.

To reproduce them all really calls for a separate book, but two are worth including here as they give a glimpse of the society's earlier days. The problem with topical references is understanding them years or even decades later. I initially thought of adding footnotes, but these could possibly have ended up as long as the ditties themselves. The solution I have chosen is to add names in square brackets where necessary for the purpose of clarification. Three pubs are also mentioned: The George & Dragon in the Ironmarket, The Compasses, which I believe was the former name of the pub on the corner of the Ironmarket and Nelson Place, now the Queen Victoria, and the Sutherland Arms near to the bottom of Priory Road and, at the time of writing, a burnt-out shell.

The first ditty was written by Alan Wright for the so-called 21st Anniversary party in 1955:

> Attend all ye who list to hear our Noble Players praise,
> I tell of the thrice famous shows put on in ancient days.
> When to the famous G & D there came from miles around
> The loveliest girls in Staffordshire, the biggest drunks in Town.
>
> 'Twas about the lousy close of a soaking autumn day,
> There came a half ton Morris Van full of speed from Pitfield way.
> To earth there sprang that noble scribe the Squire of Seagrave Place [Peter Tunstill],
> With bills and posters neatly packed in many a cardboard case.
>
> With vim and vigour, brush and paste he quickly settled down,
> To plaster Players posters onto every wall in town.
> From Higherland to Nelson Place he covered every inch.
> He even stuck a handbill over Queen Victoria's plinth.
>
> The Godwins [printers and newsagents] by the Market Cross prepare their parchment sheets
> For there behoves them to sell off the back two rows of seats.
> With his white hair unbonneted, the brave old Chairman comes.
> Before him march committee men, behind him roll the prams.
>
> Ho Burghers of Newcastle Town, know ye by all these signs
> Your famous players once again are trying to learn some lines.
> At Michaelmas they will perform a play three acts in length
> And I assure you one and all, they'll go from strength to strength.
>
> Then swift to east and swift to west the call for help was passed
> And roused in many a city bar the members of the cast.
> From Longton's lowest drinking dens, from Porthill's poshest Pubs
> Forgotten members signed the pledge and paid their last year's subs.
>
> The M.E.B. at Stoke-on-Trent right quickly shed its load
> As Mary B [Blakeman] flew speedily along the Hartshill Road.
> The Connellys came riding in from Hartwell and Cross Heath
> With a barrel on the bonnet and the baby underneath,
>
> The Emir [John Barstow] out at Endon quickly slaughtered all his swine
> And made the George and Dragon on the stroke of opening time.
> Southward from Cheshire's pleasant plains with Balance Sheet displayed
> Lord Treasurer Strachan came prancing, cautious but unafraid.

By Jaguar from Barlaston the Baron started north
But ere he reached the Muni Hall his license was endorsed.
Old Alan [Spriggs] left his hothouse flowers to Audrey's tender care.
Again we hear his battle cry "Malbrouk s'en va t'en Guerre".

Down Priory Road came William [Stevens] with tools and bags of nails.
Vida[7] at home sat sorrowing, amongst the whitewash pails.
The Masons came from Sidmouth, the Talbots heard the call,
Harden, Cotton, Showan, Devall they answered one and all.

They worked themselves to shadows, their backs are aching yet.
They did two full rehearsals and erected half a set.
The Producer got quite frantic as very well she might
But the Players proudly answered, 'twill be all right on the night.

Night sank upon the pot banks grim and in the Muni Hall,
Such night in England ne'r had been, not since the play before.
The programme sellers pulled their guns; the Stewards drew their swords
As fast from every village round the cripples came in hordes.

The deaf, the blind, the wooden legs, knock knees, cross-eyes, flat feet,
All waving complimentaries and demanding gangway seats.
The Potter left his pot to rot on Salisbury's sliphouse floor.
The Venton tilers rushed to book from Boslem and High Carr.

By lane and wide arterial road from every neighbouring shire
Bumper to nose in endless rows the P.M.T.'s on hire.
And from the Haywood's wards was heard the patter of tiny feet,
As heirs to footlight fame poured forth to hear their parent's bleat.

The Mayor and Mayoress sat in chains, the Rector on a chair,
While 'gainst the back wall Mary B was sitting in despair.
The moment comes, the Queen is played, the houselights slowly pale,
Then thunder from the staircase as the Stewards dash for ale.

A deathly silence follows, then the lights come slowly up
The Hon. Sec. parts the curtains and says "Folk you've bought a pup.
We much regret the Play is off in spite of all our toil.
The heroine's had triplets and the hero's got a boil."

The second, rather longer, ditty is a joint effort by Enid Tunstill and Bob West who looked back on the first forty years at the 40th Anniversary party on 17th January 1975. This was transcribed, in 2006, from a tape recording and unfortunately there were a few words which proved impossible to decipher:

Enid:
Tonight is the night when we let it all hang.
The Newcastle Players celebrate with a bang.
It's their fortieth year and some stories to tell
Of success and failure, of heaven and hell.

On January 17th in 1935
And thereupon the Players came alive.
Then trod the boards the very first to seek dramatic fame
And heralded the launching of proud and famous names.

We started in the Assembly Rooms and had quite a session there.
John Rowley was the producer with Jack Mason in the chair.
In days of yore with you lot here, at least excepting one,
Had hardly ever seen a stage, much less had been on one.
Brave folks like Joan [Connelly] and 'Luned [Mason] and even JFB [Barstow].
All in their prime and trying to set their inhibitions free.

When we were young [rest of line unintelligible]
If we would book seats for a play, then we would have to queue
At 6 a.m. at Godwin's shop in Cheapside in the town.
When booking opened all the stalwarts would rush down
And stand in line. And book their seats. The whole lot in one go.
If Bill was first, the rest of 'em just didn't want to know.

John Barstow's had his moments and played many a merry prank
But his clearest memory of the lot was when his mind went blank.
And many a thing we did those days we'd never dare do now,
Like dashing to The Compasses which nearly caused a row.

The men, in make-up, between scenes, went out to get a brew.
John Rowley missed two pages out. The time it fairly flew.
Then someone ran to fetch them back. They nearly died a death.
They rolled onstage, gasping out lines with frenzied, beery breath.

Our founder, dear John Rowley, had a problematic time
When on the stage he'd sometimes stand forgetting every line.
And once, when prompt in corner had dried up, his face went red.
The only words he could say, six times, were "Roses are red".

We did a lot of plays there, ending with *Nine Till Six*
Because we wore our welcome out by appearing in camiknicks.
So we went up to Saint Andrew's Hall standing at Porthill
And there, for the second time on stage, we saw Peter Tunstill.
Syd Durrant too, because the war was on and of men we were bereft.
We had to take what was offered. There were only those two left.

From there we moved to Priory Hall. It really was divine.
We felt inspired and settled down to write a pantomime.
With Cinderella on her throne, a Steventon's Venton loo
And the men as ballerinas we had a splendid do.
Ben [Devall] was the Fairy Queen and mimed while Enid [Tunstill] sang behind.
His mum was thrilled to find that her Ben had a sweet voice, so refined.

There some crazy goings-on after the curtain's fall
Like when we left 'Luned playing in the roof at Priory Hall.
We'd moved the ladder well away,
Having placed her in the rafters,
Intending then to get her down at the end of the play.

Well, after the audience had left the hall we changed our clothes
And thought at once of dashing to some place to drown our woes.
So we nipped off to the Sutherland to down a pint or two.
Hours later we wondered where Eluned had got to.

Mary [Blakeman] had joined by now and she had started to produce some.
She really knocked us into shape with methods rather gruesome.
Her first play, which she acted in, was a war one, called *No Medals*.
She still has none, but should have, Just for coping with us devils.

And so on to the Muni and of course the G & D
Where we used to gather after .. work, the better there to see
What we were doing right or wrong, and for what we'd not be blamed,
For even then dear Mary would get her senses all inflamed:
"You'll stay here until one o'clock … or until I bloody like it."

Interjection by Mary Blakeman: "I'm sorry, but it's true."

Hilary [Tindall] , of *The Brothers* fame was with us for a course.
In fact, the boys like her so much she nearly caused divorce.
She had a lot of talent and was the prettiest of misses.
The men kept lining up on stage, all eager for her kisses.

John Talbot also made his mark in a play where he wore a kilt
And vaulted over a settee back which gave it quite a tilt.
All his fans had booked front seats so that they all have a view
Of whether Scotsmen, true or ham, really wore any trews.

There never was a bloke as good, when it came to saying lines, as Denis [Connelly]
Whose delivery was really very fine. He'd play his part and in the aisles
Invariably would knock 'em.
But he had a job to say the line: "Today I have touched bottom."
Mary would make him cry with mirth, asking: "Are you through?
Or is there any other little bit you'd like to do"

One day a patron of the plays watched Denis on the stage and said:
"I used to know 'im years ago.
He used to earn a wage cleaning ferth' council. He were a mate o' mine
Yerv got 'and it to 'im. Since them days 'e's got on fine."

We did a play a play called *Viceroy Sarah* and a funny thing happened
That set an air of precedence that'll never be surpassed.
One night, before the curtain, Peter Barstow had to go
And to leave a space in the line-up would have really spoiled the show.
So Pat Mason being a mate of his, he offered to stand in
And dressed up in Peter's uniform. It cost the lad a gin.

On to the Mitch and here we've done some things to make you think,
With Denis on a pedestal and Enid on a plinth.
And Buffie [Rowley], screwed into the stage and Bob [West] boxed up with nudes.
Lying there for ages. It was really rather rude.
Paul T [Tunstill] lying on the catwalk, the only one who'd dare,
[Start of line unintelligible] . . . as if he didn't care.

Mary doing *Black Chiffon* and winning *Sentinel* acclaim.
She can't be spared to act much. It really is a shame.

Richard [Stevens], you never know these days if he'll join the ranks of prods,
Is always coming from or going to the dogs.

Rehearsals up at Pitfield House delighted us no end.
We tried hard to be good and not send Mary round the bend.
But habits die hard, as you know, and one we pandered to
Was stopping at nine thirty so as to go and down a few.

So one night, ere we settled down, Pat [Mason] placed his own alarm
Secretly under Mary's chair. Not wishing any harm
But seeking to remind her that her charges,
Strong and true men,
However keen on acting, after all, are only human.

By now we'd bought the Hartshill den for our very own.
The backstage boys work hard up there.
It's quite a home from home.

Pat's there and slaves with quite a will with one eye on the costs.
John Whittaker and George [Hurlstone], without whose help we would be lost,
Patrick [Sunderland] too, doing . . . his own thing. I'm sure he does it well,
While Ben, being all artistic, paints away like merry hell.
Bill [Stevens], with his big hammer and his heavy bag of nails,
Just walked in across the set, in spite of Mary's wails.

One day, just for publicity, they had a picture taken of members working at the den.
Who was the keenest of them all, bright-eyed and bushy-tailed?
'Twas Peter [Tunstill] in his pressed white coat, holding a brush and his whitewash pail.
Our noble scribe, though, does his whack with never a sigh or moan.
He spends hours writing minutes up or on the telephone
And selling tickets by the score and sending up our stock
By telling people how good we are.

And so onto the social side. It's really very tiring.
The committee bends its mind to things like dances, food and wine.
When a play is over and the rest begin to sag
They us on a picnic, to hunt for treasure for a gag.

Then all the cars come full of young, old, halt and lame
Mums and dads and kids and friends, all keen to play the game
And many a twisting road is found and many a twisting way
To get to the same meeting place. Some take the pretty way.

Always the clever, eager ones don't care what you do.
They'll walk off with the winners' prize and always the same two
Will be sure to get lost and come in late
Because Bill [Stevens] couldn't find where Vida had taken him on the map.

But the Players are romantic and have their true successes
When the boys pop the question and the girls choose wedding dresses.
Eventually, with Buffie's help, they extend the family tree.
We catch 'em young and they're brought to the Mitch to get rehearsal tea.
This way they rise to stardom and plum jobs fall in their lap
By getting on the beer like the other little chaps.

Girls who cut sandwiches and serve the green room tea
The wardrobe, props and prompt and ticket lady C [Ceilia Connelly],
The music man, the front-of-house, the programme sellers too,
All do their bit and do it well. They've got a job to do.

Bob:
And now it falls to me to tell you tales of yesteryear.
So take a deep breath. Have a drink. And pin back both your ears.

Do you remember *Dear Charles* and "Good God. Is that mine?"
And *Opal* of course with teabags on line.
Celebration with Denis in flat 'at.
And everyone's accent from Bacup to baht'at.

Then *Rape of the Belt* and those short sexy tunics
Which the men wore, revealing at times little blue knicks
That they'd recently purchased from Marks up in Hanley.
"Honestly, darling, they look ever so manly."

Sue Innell was cornered backstage by young Terry [Adams]
And, when she emerged, she seemed oh so red-faced
With hand marks all over her sweater.
Where we're not telling. To imagine is better.

In *Sailor Beware* those two jolly tars
And old Henry [Bob West] who threw the occasional vase
With bowler and boots. They bore him no malice
When someone said later: "He looks like Slack Alice."

I remember a one-act *While the Circus Passes*
With Pat Mason as Sam wearing dinky half glasses.
Poor Pat found it hard to remember a line.
So he took on his book and all was then fine.

George Hurlstone, an SM all fit, hale and hearty,
Stoned out of his mind at an after-play party.

Enid Tunstill and Bob West performing their ditty at the 40th Anniversary party.

    Next morning, when we were all busily working,
    George sat at the back. Some said he was shirking.
    But now we all know this just wasn't true.
    He sat at the back to be near to the loo.

    In *Someone Waiting* Dear Enid's bra
    Thought things had gone on far too far.
    Said lower cup to upper strap:
    "I think it's time we two did snap."

    Enid belted all too soon
    And hoped Mike Owens had warmed his spoon.
    She just couldn't move. She couldn't shout,
    But hope she was off before it came out.

    News of some Players like Pat Whit [Whittaker] and John
    Who've produced two new members and they're still going on.

Paddy [O'Donnell] the Pipsqueak and Kath. What a pair!
Are fine people who surely are destined to share
Success in the plays, as have Ali and Rod [Owens].
You remember the latter – the gravel pit bod.

There's Voluptuous Val [Owens], always washing her hair,
John, her old man, and Maggie and Blair [Brady].
Judy and Mick [Whewell] with tying hand all steady.
"A battery", says Judy. "He's always Eveready".

Richard Stevens, of course, with that very fine seat.
If you've been in a play, you'll remember his feet.
The smell is a strange one. The aroma is strong.
To tell you the truth, it's an 'orrible pong.

Bridget [Woolley] and Gloria [Walker], two spiffing girls,
Who've had the lads panting, heads round in whirls.
Now this is a fact and I don't want to brag.
I've seen them wink back at that lecherous stag.

There's Mary and Geoff Price. He's really a dear.
In a one-act once he played a queer.
Now, I don't believe it's true to say
He greets his friends with "What a gay day".

Christine "Copper Kettle" and Jim [Ward] the big lad
Have pushed the boat out and we're jolly glad.
They visited Edna's and Doug's [Challinor] for Sunday tea.
Jim played with Doug's organ. Seems a strange thing to me.

Paul Tunstill did well in his big play debut.
By the shape of his trousers, he'd missed in the loo.
And Terry, of course, was also a hit
Whenever he managed to get off his pitch.

Buffie has not been the same since that day
When she had the misfortune, well, that is to say,
She followed her right arm all the way round
And screwed herself down right into the ground.

Paddy is handsome with square, jutting chin.
He sometimes reminds me of dear Gungha Din.
He plays his parts well. Really quite slick
But the sight of manure makes him feel very sick.

That delightful couple, Paul Godfrey and June.
All tickled pink. They're producing quite soon.
He's frustrated we hear. They haven't a dog,
So he walks round the block and pretends it's a jog.

Enid and Bob:
And so the gang all pull their weight and go to any length
To help the Players while "We go from strength to strength".

The past's been told. The present's now.
And future Players will be told of how
Your poet laureates did their stint
And, whilst there isn't any hint
Of wishing us to go, we must
And hopefully we too will trust
In ten years time that we're all here
To celebrate our fiftieth year.

So let you hair down. Have a ball.
To Newcastle Players – Thank you, one and all.

12. The Programmes

In the early days of the society there was little recognisable uniformity in the design of our programmes. Every few plays the style would change, sometimes slightly and sometimes more radically. The only constant factor was that they were printed on quarto paper folded to give an octavo page size (8 inch x 5 inch). The price was twopence, rising to threepence in 1941. From 1943 to 1950 the price remained constant but the size and shape of the programme went through six different variations plus various colours of paper and ink.

Some semblance of uniformity was created in 1951 (*Bonaventure*) with the adoption of an 8 7/8 inch by 5 11/16 inch page size. The paper was cream and, after using green ink once, the colour of the ink was brown. This was the standard until 1962, although the price eventually went up to sixpence for full-length plays (8 pages) while remaining at threepence for one-act plays (4 pages).

1962 (*You Can't Take It With You*) saw the introduction of our familiar red white and black colour scheme and the harlequin logo, although there was no change of size or price. Peter Tunstill and Monty Slater are credited with creating the new image. In 1973 the current metric A5 size was introduced, although there was no change in overall design. The first was in fact a simple four-page programme in black and white only for a two-night performance of *AN EVENING OF ONE ACT PLAYS* in July 1973.

Our first programmes contained little more than the details of the play, sometimes with a list of past productions and, for a time, advertisements for local businesses. There were exceptions from time to time. The programmes for *Nine Till Six* (November 1942) and *Yes and No* (February 1943) for example both carried this warning and request:

A.R.P.

> In the event of an AIR RAID WARNING being received the audience will be advised and the play will proceed. A spotter will be posted, and should danger be imminent it will be announced, and the play will stop. You are advised in this event to proceed quietly to the nearest Air Raid Shelters on Car Park adjoining this building.

A selection of early Newcastle Players programmes.

> In the exigencies of 'Black Out' the ventilation is not quite as adequate as is desired and patrons are respectfully requested not to smoke to excess.

In the case of *Yes and No* it was felt necessary to add the following explanation:

> In the present emergency the Players desire to point out that the Bread and Cakes used during the play are provided by the members of the cast, who after the Show return same home for consumption.

The AIR RAID WARNING note was repeated for all performances up to February 1944 but without the request to refrain from smoking to excess.

Jupiter Laughs (October 1949) was our first play at the Municipal Hall, Newcastle and this occasioned a rather longer note in the programme:

> This is the first time we have played in the Municipal Hall Theatre. It is our intention that it shall not be the last but firm as this intention is, we are entirely in your hands.
>
> For over twenty years now the Newcastle Players have produced two plays each year, sometimes we have managed three and always we have endeavoured to please and entertain you.
>
> Some of our 'regulars' will, of course, recall the plays put on at Marsh St. Assembly Rooms before the war – since then we have, alas, been 'pushed around' but now we have embarked on a bigger venture by coming to this Theatre and we need your support so that our audiences will be large ones and in the fullness of time we shall be able to have our own little Theatre which in truth will be yours.
>
> With this in view then we have included with this programme a small card for your especial use. If you would care to be on our mailing list just fill in your name and address and hand the card to one of our members on your way out. There is no obligation but it will mean that you will receive our notices of forthcoming plays and have an opportunity of booking your seats early.

A similar but shorter note, dealing only with the mailing list, appeared in the programme for the next play, *Pink String and Sealing Wax*, in May 1950. From then on programmes started to contain small items on an irregular basis: a foreword from the Chairman (*Bonaventure* – April 1951), a tribute to John Rowley (*Home at Seven* – April 1952), a note about the historical background of the play (*Viceroy Sarah* – November 1952) and so on, including invitations to patrons to add their names and addresses our mailing list and, increasingly

THE NEWCASTLE PLAYERS

"BONAVENTURE"

A play by Charlotte Hastings.

MUNICIPAL HALL THEATRE, NEWCASTLE

11, 12, 13, 14, APRIL 1951

PROGRAMME - THREEPENCE

This was the style of programme used from 1951 to 1962

more frequently, to "young men and women interested in the theatre" to apply for membership of the society.

In November 1958 we moved to the Mitchell Memorial Theatre, Hanley and the programme for *The House by the Lake* contained a note explaining the change of venue:

> THE Newcastle Players would be unable to function as a society without the excellent support from you our patrons. It is only natural therefore that your welfare and comfort should be of primary interest to us and whilst we all regret leaving Newcastle we are presenting our plays at the Mitchell Memorial Theatre, Hanley, in the future, because it is ideally suited to us and offers greater comfort and facilities for you.
>
> We sincerely believe that you will benefit from our move and trust that it will be justified by your continued support.

With the move to Hanley we started to "respectfully remind our patrons that smoking is not permitted in the auditorium". Nowadays it is not permitted anywhere in the theatre building. Things have moved on a long way since patrons were "respectfully requested not to smoke to excess".

In 1964 (*Something to Hide*) we rather gingerly faced up to the problem of the dreaded sweet paper rustler with a little poem:

"The Sad Ballad of Jim"

> There was a young lady called Jane
> And to a theatre she came,
> Her newly wed husband called Jim
> He also deigned to come in,
> Bringing sweets and chocolates to eat
> He nipped smartly into his seat.
>
> When soon the curtain did rise
> Young Jim had such a surprise,
> The shouts the boos and the hisses
> Directed at him and his Mrs.
> Presenting to Jane the sweets so proudly
> He'd opened the wrappers far too loudly.
>   ANON CIRCA 1964

The Harlequin and banner style was used, with some slight changes, until 2004.

But it was not until 1981 (*Suspect* – 30 March to 4 April) that we began to include short articles on various subjects, but mainly our Theatre Workshop in Hartshill. The first of these described the financial problems we were facing following the City of Stoke-on-Trent's creation of the Hartshill Conservation Area and our need to raise a large sum of money to restore the outside of the building in accordance with the terms of the conservation area.

The first picture appeared in November 1983 (*Lloyd George Knew My Father*). It was a self-portrait of Horace Barks, former Lord Mayor of Stoke-on-Trent, prominent figure in North Staffordshire public life, leading Esperantist and a valued friend of the Newcastle Players. His letters to the Newcastle Players were often written in a mixture of Standard English, Pottery dialect and Esperanto. They were always a joy to read. The last one we received was written on the back of the only piece of paper he could put his hand on at the time which was the self-portrait opposite. He said 'I never did like it anyway'. We liked it. More than that, we treasured it as a reminder of a man, whom we sadly missed, and we used it to illustrate our tribute to him after his death that year.

1984 was our Golden Jubilee Year and the programme for our production of *Outside Edge* in November was a radical departure from anything that had gone before. The format was A4 – the only time so far that we have used such a large format; there were sixteen pages; and it was full of photographs and articles plus five pages of advertisements. In many ways it was a miniature version of this book, although only covering fifty years, with articles on the backstage crew and our theatre workshop, past plays and the theatres or halls in which they had been presented, a tribute to our founder, John Rowley, and photographs of the cast and our Life Members.

All our programmes since then have included photographs of the cast and a wealth of articles related to the play or the society.

The new millennium saw the beginning of a change to the cover of our programmes. First came a move away from a standard typeface (font) for the title of the play, which from May 2000 (*Funny Money*) attempted to reflect the nature of the play. In November 2002 (*The Exorcism*) the current lower case style of **newcastle**_players_ first appeared. And November 2004 (*It Runs in the Family*) we abandoned the banner which had been held by the harlequin for the past forty-three years. It was replaced with a proscenium arch and curtains framing the title and other details of the play and a picture illustrating what the play was about, the latter the work of our talented artist member Sylvia Fisher.

Horace Barks (self-portrait)

For the two productions in our 2004-2005 70th Anniversary season ((*It Runs in the Family* and *The Ghost Train*) the format went up from A5 (148 x 210 mm) to a trimmed variant (170 x 245 mm) of B5, similar to that frequently used in the professional theatre, but with *How The Other Half Loves* (November 2005) it returned to our familiar A5 size.

50 Years—93 Plays

With a record of 93 productions (not counting several evenings of one act plays) during our first fifty years it is a difficult task to select some for mention and to omit others. We all have our own favourites, whether we are members of the society or members of the audience. Certainly at the end of every performance—and we hope that tonight's will be no exception—someone says to us: "It's the best you've ever done".

It might be assumed that the Newcastle Players' own favourites are those which we have done twice: "Ladies in Retirement" in 1945 and 1968, "Bonaventure" in 1951 and 1982, and "My Three Angels" in 1959 and 1981. But there are others which we would like to repeat but for one reason or another cannot.

All we can say is that we have enjoyed presenting every single one of the plays we have staged since 1935 and we hope that our audiences have enjoyed them just as much. Those which are featured on these two pages have been chosen entirely at random. We hope that these few illustrations bring back happy memories.

A full list of our 93 full length productions and the years in which they occurred can be found overleaf.

"THE GHOST TRAIN"
Newcastle Players' First Performance

For their inaugural dramatic performance the Newcastle Players showed considerable enterprise in submitting "The Ghost Train," which depends so much for its effect upon the generation of the right atmosphere of eeriness and the delineation of character.

The success which did, in fact, attend their presentation of this popular "thriller" at Newcastle yesterday is thus all the more creditable, and promises well for the future of this young society, which aims at providing good dramatic fare and affording scope for the development of the acting talent in the ancient borough.

Yesterday's production was satisfying in every way. Mr. A. Ridley's three-act mystery play called for scenery and effects much more elaborate than are normally attempted on the amateur stage, and the producer, Mr. John W. Rowley, is to be congratulated on his achievement, and on the excellence of the team which was responsible for the various departments of the work behind the scenes.

NOTABLE SUCCESSES

On the stage, Mr. John W. Rowley had the leading role of Teddie Deakin, the detective who masks his serious task by the pose of frivolous futility, and he gave a clever performance.

As Julia, the woman crook who feigns madness in order to scare away the stranded passengers waiting at the "Ghost Train's" station, Miss Rose Moran was splendid, while the other characters were all well portrayed. As Miss Bourne, the nervous spinster, Miss Marjorie Brown gave a well-studied performance, Mr. W. T. Hand was convincing as the stationmaster, and John G. Walsh handled the part of the pseudo doctor with skill. Miss Mary Kent, Miss Cecily Tinsdill, and Messrs. Denis Connelly, Henry J. Barker, Gerald C. Tinsdill and Bernard J. Wright all made their parts definite contributions to the success of the whole.

The Players, whose President is Dr. R. A. Keane, and whose Chairman is Mr. J. M. Mason, received a gratifying measure of support, among the large audience being the Mayor of Newcastle (Mr. J. Bentley).

Above and opposite: Two pages from our programme for "Outside Edge" – our first magazine style programme – in November 1984

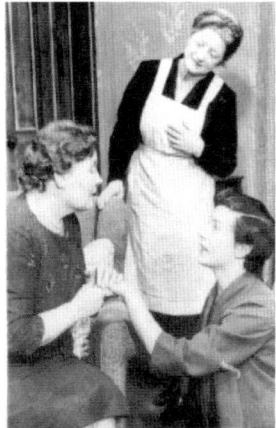

Players' successful 'Cure'

NEWCASTLE PLAYERS have entered Coronation Street territory for their latest production in their Golden Jubilee year.

Like the famous television soap opera, Walter Greenwood's comedy "The Cure for Love," which opened at the Mitchell Memorial Theatre, Hanley, last night is set in Salford, but in this case the period is towards the end of the Second World War.

The flak which Sergeant Jack Hardacre has suffered from El Alamein onwards is nothing compared with the romantic and ... hassles he has to endure on ... return home.

It all ma... write as a native Mancunian), but this was more than offset by the standard of acting and sense of ensemble.

As the compliant, long-suffering Jack Hardacre, Bob West gave a beautifully-gauged performance splendidly aided and abetted by the two women in his life, Janet Banks as Milly Southern, the self-assured, sophisticated southerner and apple of his eye, and ... Ardle who, as Janey Jenkins, his ... and a millstone round his neck, ... lly and facially reminiscent of Dora

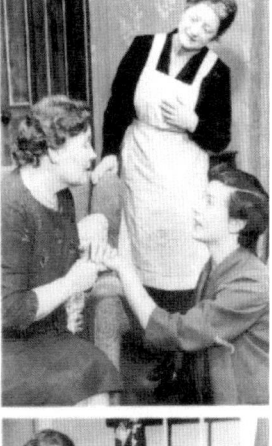

... n had imposing dramatic pre... he formidable matriarch Sarah ... did Jim Ward on the role of her ... ublican, Harry Lancaster.

... other notable performances ... Beardmore as the busybody

Players make ideal choice

LAST YEAR when I reviewed "My Three ..." I said how ... ns to pre-...

fidently to the back of the well-filled auditorium, and the set is immaculate and ... degree of ... exemplary. ... Yet their ... does not en... nium arch ... producer ... Players' ... arrangem... g a outstand... ng how eff... hat an eve... all just a ... olid Ther... hich here, ... ods. have ... , then, nigh... layers.

Players score a hit with farce

A COLLECTION of oddball characters thrown together by fate in a Fawlty Towers type hotel provides

Opposite page:
Top: *You Can't Take it with You* (1962).
Bottom: *Interference* (1936).
This page:
Top left: *Therese* (1963). Top right: *Black Chiffon* (1962). Centre right: *The Amorous Prawn* (1975). Bottom right: *Spring at Marino* (1972).

Our current programme style.

13. Festivals and Awards

Some groups seem to exist purely to compete in drama festivals and to win awards. So much so, in fact, that The Mitchell Memorial Theatre Users Group introduced a rule in 2006 that entries in its annual one-act play festival must "include details of the group's existence for 1 year minimum with public performances." Newcastle Players would have no difficulty complying with this requirement, since, for over seventy years, we have existed purely to provide entertainment through public performances while, of course, getting a great deal of enjoyment out of it ourselves.

In the 1960s there was some talk of providing opportunities for newer and younger members to take the stage by setting up a special section which might take part in drama festivals. Various possible names were discussed: "Newcastle Players Two" was not approved, but "The Younger Newcastle Players" was considered a possibility. In the end it seems nothing came of this and it was not until our 2004/2005 season that we entered a festival – The Mitchell Memorial Theatre Full Length Play Festival – and this did not involve anything more than providing facilities for an adjudicator to view one of the regular performances of our productions.

Although this was the thirtieth time the festival had been held, it was the first time the Newcastle Players had been eligible to enter. Previously the festival had only been open to Youth and Community Groups, but it was now open to all "amateur drama societies whose performances take place at the Mitchell Memorial Theatre".

Trophies won

The first time we entered there were eleven awards in total. Three of them did not apply to us, but we won three of the others plus a fourth for an individual member. In addition individual members were nominated for two of the other awards.

All the awards received were for *The Ghost Train*. The first time Jim Ward went up on the stage at the awards ceremony it was to collect THE RAY MARTIN TROPHY (for Presentation). We also received THE MITCHELL

Chris Wilkinson receiving his trophy for the "Best Performance under 21 Years of Age" from Chairman Jim Ward before the start of a play-reading ("Present Laughter" by Noël Coward) at the Oxford Arms, May Bank on Tuesday, 14th June 2005.

TROPHY (for the Best Non-Musical Performance) and THE CHARLES RAINES MEMORIAL TROPHY (as the overall Runner-Up in the festival).

Earlier in the season adjudicator Paul Fowler had said that *It Runs in the Family* was the best non-musical performance he had ever seen at The Mitch, so the adjudicators must have thought that we went one better with *The Ghost Train*.

On the individual front Chris Wilkinson won the MOW COP PLAYERS 30th ANNIVERSARY TROPHY (for Best Performance Under 21 Years of Age) for his portrayal of Charles Murdock in *The Ghost Train* – a performance which, said the adjudicator, showed great maturity.

The following season both our productions won awards: *How The Other Half Loves* won THE RAY MARTIN TROPHY (for Presentation) and *Because of the Lockwoods* THE MITCHELL TROPHY (for the Best Non-Musical Performance).

Trophies donated

It is said to be better to give than to receive and in recent years we have given two trophies.

At our Annual General Meeting in 2000 it was proposed that the Newcastle Players should sponsor a trophy for the annual Newcastle-under-Lyme Festival for Music, Speech and Drama and in 2001 an elegant trophy (pictured top right) was purchased and suitably engraved. It is dedicated to the memory of Mary Blakeman and goes each year to the winner of Class 31: Solo Drama – 9 to 10 years. The first winner was Hannah Morris of Blythe Bridge whose own choice test piece was a dramatised extract from *Jane Eyre* by Charlotte Brontë and Hannah received the trophy from our then Chairman Buffie Rowley.

After becoming eligible to enter The Mitchell Memorial Theatre Full Length Play Festival in our 70th Anniversary season – and doing rather well in it ourselves – we decided to donate a trophy to be known as the NEWCASTLE PLAYERS 70TH ANNIVERSARY TROPHY (for the best individual performance by an actress). This is pictured bottom right. The first winner of the new trophy was Diane Collings for her performance as Christine Hammond in The New Peoples Theatre production of *Victim* by Don West.

14. Spreading A Word

In 1984 we celebrated the fiftieth anniversary of the founding of the Newcastle Players with a production of *Outside Edge* by Richard Harris – a play which subsequently became very well known after being turned into a television series and which was still being toured professionally as recently as 2004.

As mentioned a couple of times earlier, one of the things we did to mark the special occasion was to publish our first ever magazine-style programme and the only one we've ever done in A4 format. One of the other things we did for the first time ever was to include in the programme the following, rather wordy, invitation to the audience to come backstage after the performance:

> To stage a production such as the one you are seeing tonight requires much more than a number of actors of the right age and sex with the ability to interpret properly the intentions of the author of the play. Important as these people are, they are just the visible tip of the theatrical iceberg. They could not perform without the support of a bigger, largely unseen and frequently unacknowledged group of people.
>
> As we celebrate our Golden Jubilee it is fitting that we should pay tribute to the producers, scenery designers and builders, people who take care of properties and costumes, lighting and sound, changes of scenery and special effects, front of house staff, box office and ticket sellers, not forgetting the caretakers and other members of the theatre staff who ensure that everything is in good order for our audiences. All these are just as important as the actors and without them we would not have been able to stage *Outside Edge* or the other 92 plays the Newcastle Players have presented over the last fifty years.
>
> The process starts with a dedicated committee which reads several plays before selecting the one which will be put on. Rarely the choice is easy. More often publishers' lists are gone over again and again and dozens of plays have to be read before the right one is found. For, unlike the professional theatre, amateurs have to match the play to the members available at the time.
>
> However, once the play has been decided upon, everything swings into motion. Actors begin rehearsing, scenery is designed and built, properties, furniture and costumes are acquired or hired, publicity gets

under way and, for our more successful productions, more than two thousand tickets are sold.

The front of house staff comes into direct contact with our audiences. The work of the scenery building team is described elsewhere in this special souvenir programme. But what goes on backstage is – or should be – unseen and unheard.

This week we are making a break with a fifty-year tradition. For the first time and probably the only time we are inviting you our audience to come backstage after the show to see something of what goes on there and to meet not only the stage manager and his crew but possibly also one or two members of the cast before they retire to their dressing rooms to change out of costume and remove their make-up.

Numbers are of necessity limited, since it would not be possible to accommodate the whole audience on the stage. But if you would like to take advantage of this invitation please tell one of the stewards.

Quite a few members of the audience took advantage of this offer and came round onto the stage after the final curtain. It gave them the opportunity to see the set from the actors' point of view, to see the minute space from which the prompter operates, to talk to the actors about their parts and so on.

There was, however, one unforeseen and unfortunate consequence.

The platform floor of the cricket pavilion was only intended to carry the weight of two or three actors and actresses at any one time. One evening, though, with about twenty members of the audience standing on it, the platform collapsed. The stage manager had to spend much of the next day repairing the damage and, for the rest of the week, we were very careful how many people were allowed on it at any one time. What's more, we haven't repeated the invitation to the audience to come backstage en masse either.

On the other hand, the response we received to the *Outside Edge* invitation did indicate to us that many people have an interest in the theatre which goes beyond just seeing plays. More than one backstage visitor commented: "Oh, I would never have the nerve to perform in public." But there were also questions like "how do you remember all those words?" or "what exactly does the producer do?" and "where do you get your furniture from?"

This gave us the idea that people might like to hear something of what is involved in putting on a theatrical production. From this evolved a talk about

Geoff Price, Jim Ward and John Talbot on the "Outside Edge" platform which collapsed.

the amateur theatre in general and the Newcastle Players in particular. It's called *A Word on Plays* and since the mid-eighties we have been giving it to groups such as the Women's Institute, Townswomen's Guild, Rotary Club, Housewives' Circles, Church Groups and Fellowships, to name but a few, and we are prepared to travel anywhere within North Staffordshire and South Cheshire to do so.

It began as a fairly short talk – about ten minutes long – which Paul Godfrey gave to his Rotary Club. This was then developed into a talk lasting between 45 minutes and an hour, which is the length groups generally want.

Originally there was a team of three: Paul Godfrey, John Talbot and myself (Geoff Price) – all giving slightly different versions of the talk, as we added our own anecdotes to illustrate the points we were making. After a time I found myself doing most of the talks and, when I had done it about fifty times, I appealed for some help. Jim Ward came to the rescue and said he would take over "for a year or so". To date he has been doing it for at least seventeen years. I haven't heard Jim's talk but I imagine that by now it is very different from mine. For one thing he uses slides to illustrate what he is talking about, whereas I don't.

I still give the talk from time to time. Sometimes it's because Jim has taken a booking, which can be as much as two years in advance, and subsequently finds that he has another event he must attend. He then asks me to step in. On other occasions it's when somebody I know asks if I will give the talk. Once, when this happened, I was surprised to see Jim in the audience. He was equally surprised to see that I was the speaker. He had been invited along by someone who was trying to persuade him to become a member of the particular club, but he hadn't been told who the speaker was.

If you belong to an organisation that would be interested in hearing *A Word on Plays* you can usually find out who to contact for details in our latest programme. Alternatively use the *Contact Us* section of our website at http://www.newcastleplayers.org.uk.

We would be happy to hear from you and happier still to come and talk to you.

15. The Newcastle Players on Other Platforms

Reference in previous chapter to the platform which collapsed brings to mind the fact that the Newcastle Players have occasionally performed on other "platforms", although the stage has always been our real home.

In August 1946, which was during our "fallow" period between St Andrews Porthill and St Giles Parish Hall, an Extraordinary General Meeting was held, the purpose of which appears to have been the handing over of the chairmanship from Ernest Butterworth to John Legge and the taking over by R. J. Pringle Brown of the vice-chairmanship vacated by John Legge.

Another item discussed was the staging of some one-act plays which had been in rehearsal to fill the gap created by having no hall to perform full-length productions in and the minutes contain the following intriguing note:

> M. Blakeman suggested that it might be advisable to put two on in one night and Mr Rowley suggested that the film of the Newcastle Players might be shown. This lead to a discussion regarding the completion of the film upon which all members should be included if possible.

There is no mention of this film anywhere else and no indication of what it contained or what happened to it.

A few years later, however, Stoke-on-Trent Amateur Cine Society asked if we could provide some actresses for their next film and at our 1954 Annual General Meeting it was reported that the film society had won an award for its film *Handle for Scandal* in which Eluned Mason and Olive Wright had appeared and that the film society was looking forward to our future cooperation.

We were not to appear on film again though (or video or DVD) until many years later.

In the autumn of 1967 we learnt that John Abberley, who had been the *Evening Sentinel's* theatre correspondent for some time, was leaving the paper to join the BBC, or to be more accurate, BBC Radio Stoke-on-Trent (to give it the title it used until the mid-1980s) which was due to go on air early the next year. The Executive Committee decided to form an ad hoc committee to keep in close touch with John to see if the Newcastle Players could be involved in radio broadcasting and one-act plays. However, shortly after the new station began broadcasting we learnt that another local radio station, Radio Merseyside, had fallen foul of the actors' union Equity because it had used amateurs for one of its very popular radio serials. In view of this we did not pursue our idea any further.

Nearly thirty years later we and other amateur societies were approached to provide extras for an episode of a Central Television series called *It's Your Shout*. As a result four members of the Newcastle Players appeared before their biggest audience ever – and they didn't have a single line between them. On Sunday 17th December 1995 Humphrey Gawthrop, Di West, John Talbot and Dennis Layton were seen as members of the public in an episode of *It's Your Shout* which had been filmed at Hanley Town Hall the previous Wednesday afternoon. The scene was a courtroom and Humphrey, Di, John and Dennis appeared whenever the lawyers for the defence and prosecution were on camera. Members of other local societies were also there but were much less prominent – with one exception: Brenda Swancott, a non-acting member of The Rep was roped in at the last moment to replace a member of the jury who had failed to turn up. Quite a lot was seen – and heard – of Brenda during the jury's deliberations.

A more prominent part was played in a television series by Janet Mulliner in 1999.

"My fiancé Robert Vaughan and I wanted to do something a bit unusual for our wedding," said Janet at the time, "and a friend suggested getting married on the stage in view of our interest in the theatre."

Janet and Robert would have preferred a theatre in North Staffordshire but in fact the nearest theatre with the appropriate licence was the Theatre Royal in Bath. Built in 1805, totally refurbished in the 1980s and widely considered to be one of the most beautiful theatres in the country, it was the first theatre in the country to be granted a license to perform wedding ceremonies from the stage.

So, not only the Mulliner and Vaughan families but also a hundred or so friends including members of the Newcastle Players made the 280 mile round trip to attend. The ceremony was conducted by Bath Registrar Judy Stone on

Robert and Janet are married on the stage of the Theatre Royal, Bath and the ceremony is filmed by a television cameraman.

the set of the Royal National Theatre's touring production of *Private Lives* by Noël Coward.

As if that was not enough, Robert and Janet's wedding and the lead up to it, including references to Janet's involvement in Newcastle Players and Audley Players productions, were featured in a Central ITV series called *Love & Marriage* about people getting married under unusual circumstances.

It was not until 2004 the Newcastle Players as such were the exclusive subject of a DVD. It was made by Professor Ray Johnson of Staffordshire University's Faculty of Arts, Media and Design and three of his students. Entitled *This Is Your Half-Hour Call,* it was filmed during the last half-hour or so before curtain-up of the Friday performance of our production of *A Party to Murder*. The four cameras captured all the action, preparations, conversation and mini-panics behind the scenes and front-of-house – dipping into relevant conversations from each throughout the run-up to the performance. The film ends as the curtains open, and we hear some final comments from the play's director, Ann McArdle.

Ray Johnson filming Ann McArdle in the foyer of the Mitchell Memorial Theatre just before the start of the Friday performance of "A Party to Murder".

Producer Ray Johnson describes the film as "a continuous four-camera timeline showing the final preparations before curtain-up of a typical amateur drama production at the Mitchell Memorial Theatre, Hanley". It is now part of the Staffordshire Film Archive. The archive is a collection of film media relating to the West Midlands region. It includes local archival collections associated with industries in the area, providing a unique perspective on the social history of the region. Some of the material in the collection dates from the early twentieth century, but Professor Johnson is adding to it all the time and he felt that the strong amateur theatre tradition in North Staffordshire deserved a place in it, hence *This is Your Half-Hour Call*.

To purchase a copy of the DVD visit our website at http://www.newcastleplayers.org.uk and click on 'news'. Then scroll down to STAFFORDSHIRE FILM ARCHIVE.

16. The Newcastle Players and The Media

Generally speaking the Newcastle Players have had a very good relationship with the media and we have valued the support we have received over the years.

The local press has always been dominated by the *Sentinel* in its various guises: *Evening Sentinel, Staffordshire Weekly Sentinel, The Sentinel* and, more recently, *Sentinel Sunday* plus, for a time, its magazine *The Way We Were* and its associated free sheet *The Advertiser*. Other publishers have attempted to gain a foothold in the North Staffordshire market, but none has been capable of staying the course.

The *Sentinel*'s complimentary remarks about our early productions have been quoted in an earlier chapter and its reviews have always been fair, although there was a point in the mid-60s when some of our members thought otherwise. The offending item was the review of our production of *Something to Hide* which appeared in the *Evening Sentinel* of 13th May 1964 under the headline WHAT A PITY – SUCH A WASTE OF TALENT. Reading the review over forty years later it is clear that it was the play that the reviewer found bad and, if he was criticising the Newcastle Players, it was for choosing a poor play, not for the way we performed it, for his piece contained the following comment:

> What made the evening doubly heart-breaking was that the acting and the production and the set were so good. I wondered why so much time, care and talent had been wasted when it could have been used in so many better plays.

Some of our senior members were so incensed at what they saw as a slur against our integrity that they vowed never to invite a *Sentinel* reviewer again. Fortunately more moderate opinions and common sense prevailed and it was not long before the paper was again being invited to send a reviewer.

In the early days reviews tended to be quite wordy. The review of *The Barretts of Wimpole Street* in November 1935 was about 1000 words long, not counting the headline OUTSTANDING SUCCESS OF NEWCASTLE PLAYERS and sub-headline NOTABLE PERFORMANCE OF "THE BARRETTS OF WIMPOLE STREET" which stretched across two columns.

The Sentinel's review of "Because of the Lockwoods" (April 2006) was accompanied by a photograph occupying more space than the review itself.

In addition to the actual review of the play itself it listed everybody connected with the production including the members "The Players' String Quartet" which "gave selections during the evening".

Styles change. These days space in the news pages is at a premium and reviews will generally be no more than a couple of hundred words long, although occasionally the review will be accompanied by an eye-catching photo which may occupy as much space as, if not more than, the actual words.

Today's paper contains more feature type articles and we have been very fortunate in the amount of free publicity that we have received in this way in recent years. We can usually count a feature in *The Sentinel*'s entertainment supplement which normally appears on Fridays. This is will be at least half a page and sometimes will stretch to a full page. There may also be other items linked to our production featuring members of the cast or back-up crew in articles about eating out, holidays, favourite walks, pets and so on.

Probably the earliest example of a long feature article appeared in the now defunct CITY TIMES of 9th March 1960. Under the headline **Players look back to their early days** it reviewed the twenty-five years since our first production of *The Ghost Train* in January 1935 and up to and including our first year or so at the Mitchell Memorial Theatre.

Now we can look back on nearly three times as long as that and more recently (June 2003) there was a three-page article in the *Sentinel*'s magazine *The Way We Were* based on an interview with Buffie Rowley and myself (Geoff Price)

Top:
The City
Times, 9th
March 1960.

Centre:
Amateur Stage,
March 2005.

Bottom:
The Way We Were,
June 2003

by local historian Mervyn Edwards. Then in 2005 the society occupied a whole page in the national magazine *Amateur Stage* with article in its March issue about our seventieth anniversary by Moira Hammond.

That was not the first time we had been featured in *Amateur Stage*. In 1993 we were invited by the editor to submit a contribution to the magazine's regular feature *The Play Produced*. The subject was our production of *Deadly Nightcap* by Francis Durbridge which we had staged in November 1992 and the result was a 2000 word article by John Talbot discussing various aspects of the play such as the plot, casting, rehearsals, scenery, lighting, properties, special requirements and problems. As a postscript to the actual article John commented that for reasons entirely unconnected with *Deadly Nightcap* we had carried out some market research in the form of an audience questionnaire during the run of the play. Many of our patrons took the opportunity to add comments such as: "Fantastic performance of DEADLY NIGHTCAP! More like that please!!"

In 1998 we joined the National Operatic and Dramatic Association (NODA) and since then we have enjoyed a very good relationship with editor of its quarterly magazine *noda NATIONAL NEWS,* John Slim. There have not been any major features on the Newcastle Players in it as yet, but John does keep his eye on our members' bulletin (see next chapter) and from time to time he picks up the odd item from it and uses it in some way in his magazine.

Local radio came on the scene in North Staffordshire in 1968 when BBC Radio Stoke (originally known by the longer title of BBC Radio Stoke-on-Trent) came on air. As mentioned in the previous chapter we had some thoughts about providing amateur actors for drama programmes, but that idea came to naught. On the other hand the station has given us considerable coverage over nearly forty years. Unfortunately, such is the nature of broadcasting that the majority of the interviews that took place were heard once and then lost for ever. Certainly in the early days recording facilities were not as widely available as they are now.

Most of our interviews took place in Radio Stoke's studios in Hanley, usually live and sometimes involving members getting up early, doing the interview when they would normally be having breakfast at home and then afterwards going on to their place of work. Sometimes though a Radio Stoke reporter would come to us, as happened in November 1996 when Barbara Adams did her afternoon programme from our workshop and was taken, on air, on a tour of the premises by Pat Mason. Fortunately Pat arranged for that to be recorded

BBC Radio Stoke journalist Helen Thomas, who is also a Newcastle Players member, interviews John Hough on air at the workshop.

and a copy, omitting the various unrelated items that filled out the half-hour programme, is now in our sound archives.

The workshop featured again more recently when our plans for refurbishing the building were discussed on air shortly after eight o'clock one morning by workshop manager John Hough interviewed by one of our members, Helen Thomas, who is also a BBC Radio Stoke journalist.

17. Communicating with Our Members, Our Patrons and the Public at Large

Communicating with members in the early days of the society was probably quite easy and more than likely by word of mouth. After all there were only three dozen members (see page 2) and, although not everybody had a telephone in those days, they presumably all attended the same church so would see each other quite regularly.

Over the years the society acquired more members and, although the nucleus still lived in Newcastle, there were others from further afield. The 1955 ditty on pages 86 and 87 refers to Longton, Hartwell, Endon, Barlaston and an unspecified location in Cheshire. Nowadays we could add Cumbria, Devon and Spain to name those who live furthest away. Clearly some other form of communicating with members was called for particularly as membership grew to around a hundred, where it seems to have stayed for quite some time.

Initially such communications would appear to have been done by circular letter. Few of these have survived, although one from 1953 is reproduced on the next page. There is, however, the following comment in the minutes of an Executive Committee meeting in December 1952:

> The Sec proposed that instead of circularising each event separately the Society should issue a Monthly Bulletin to members and this was approved by the committee.

However, as the circular overleaf shows, such letters were still being used at least a year later.

Nowadays we regularly communicate with our members through the *Newcastle Players BULLETIN*, which comes out roughly every six to eight weeks. It first appeared in 1958. Unfortunately the first issue seems to have sunk without a trace but we know from the minutes of the May 1958 Executive Committee meeting that it gave "details of the new play [presumably *The House by the Lake* – GHP] and our reason for moving to the Mitchell Memorial Theatre." A copy of the second issue has survived and this is reproduced on pages 125 and 126.

The Newcastle Players

Hon. Sec. :	Chairman	Hon. Treas.
ALAN G. WRIGHT,	J. R. LEGGE, Esq.	H. M. STRACHAN,
25, Howard Place,	Gladstone Villa,	The White House,
Newcastle, Staffs.	Victoria Road,	Alsager, Cheshire.
'Phone 65219.	Newcastle, Staffs.	Phone Alsager 365
	Phone 67540	

7th December, 1953.

Dear Player,

    An Extraordinary General Meeting will be held at The Castle Hotel, Newcastle, on Sunday December 13th at 8 o'clock p.m.

    There is a chance that The Society may be able to acquire premises suitable for conversion to a Little Theatre but before making any offer the Executive wish the whole problem of 'a home of our own' to be discussed frankly and fully in General Meeting.

    When considering this matter there are several important aspects to be borne in mind including:-

    (a) It will probably mean two years or more of hard work for us all, before the building is fully adapted and this will be in addition to that entailed in our productions. They must go on to raise the necessary funds.

    (b) When the Theatre is complete we shall have to put on four or even five productions each year to cover overheads.

    Please consider this matter carefully and do your best to come to the meeting. If you cannot, it would help if I could have your views in writing before next Sunday.

    Yours faithfully,
        ALAN G. WRIGHT,
          Hon.Secretary.

The subjects covered by the early bulletins – details of the next play, play readings, news of members and social events – still provide the staple material of the bulletin more than 400 issues later.

What has changed is the style of presentation. At first the main bulletins were issued by the secretary with occasional issues interspersed here and there by

The Newcastle Players

Honorary Secretary:
F. A. TUNSTILL,
Blithe Cottage,
29, Tavistock Crescent,
Newcastle, Staffs.
Phone 69671

Chairman:
J. R. LEGGE, Esq.
Gladstone Villas,
Victoria Road,
Newcastle, Staffs.
Phone 67540

Honorary Treasurer:
H. M. STRACHAN,
The White House,
Alsager, Cheshire.
Phone : Alsager 395

25th August, 1958.

BULLETIN NO. 2.

Dear Member,

Mailing List.

Now that we are going to the Mitchell Memorial Theatre, Hanley, it is suggested that if members care to send me the names and addresses of their patrons, the usual leaflet which will announce details of our move to Hanley and of the new play will be posted to them and thus supplement our existing mailing list. Please let me have names and addresses not later than the 30th September.

Play Readings.

Three play readings have been arranged for the Season and they will be held at the Arts Centre, Newcastle. Please make a note of these dates in your diary:
Tuesday, October 14th
Tuesday, January 27th.
Tuesday, February 24th.

One Act Plays.

The Casting Committee have arranged to present two one act plays to give "untried" members the opportunity of trying out their abilities as producers, stage managers, actors and actresses. Mary Blakeman and Bill Stevens are members of this committee and with the others feel this to be a constructive and instructive programme for the Players.
The Parish Hall, Priory Road, Newcastle, has been booked for Tuesday, December 16th and the evening will take the form of a social gathering. Further details will be notified later but book the date now.

Annual Dance.

Our Annual Dinner Dance is booked for Friday, 5th December at the Grand Hotel, Hanley. All the arrangements are in the capable hands of the Social Committee.

"The House by the Lake."

The members pre-booking night will be Tuesday, November 4th at the Castle Hotel, Newcastle at 7 p.m. Book this important date.

P.T.O.

the social committee, publicity officer or ticket secretary. They were usually in the form of a personal letter. They started with "Dear Member" and ended "Yours sincerely" followed by the signature of the author of that particular issue.

Vouchers and details will be sent to you in good time and we look forward to bumper sales for our debut at the Mitchell Memorial Theatre.

REAL news from the "social" side!!

"Sparks" Alan Keeling gives us the real "shock" by taking upon himself, on August 15th, a wife - our very hard working member Marjorie Evans.

We have at last made an honest member of John Talbot who, on August 23rd, married Joy Cooke - and what a cook!

Number 3 coming up! Mary Grant too was married on August 23rd to Denis Pickford.

Our warmest congratulations go to them all.

"STORK" Department.

Some members are not Backes to come forward.

To those not yet blessed with a fine son and heir - see Ray and Marie and N(e)il Desperandum.

Be a regular reader of Uncle Peter's Gossip Column and keep right up to date - there is more "stork" news on the way.

What a Dramatic Society!

Changes of Addresses.

For those who like to keep their Mailing List up to date, please note the following:-

Honorary Treasurer, Hedley Strachan, and Win have left Alsager and are in a temporary flat at Tunstall pending their move to Bournemouth next year. Those who have not paid their subscriptions to him now know why he had to sell his house! His new address for communications is:-

c/o, The Midland Bank Limited,
TUNSTALL,
Stoke-on-Trent. TELEPHONE: 87839.

Mr. & Mrs. J.H.Talbot will be at 38, Clumber Avenue, Newcastle (Telephone 69025) until their new house is ready.

Mr. & Mrs. Alan Keeling will reside at 2A, Albert Street, Newcastle (Telephone 64600).

Mrs. Pickford's address will be 20, High Street, May Bank, Newcastle.

Yours sincerely,
Peter Tunstill,
HONORARY SECRETARY.

With various people or committees issuing their own bulletins as they felt fit there were times when they seemed to be dropping through members' letter boxes thick and fast. In 1968 the treasurer reported that the cost of bulletins was rising considerably due to the increased cost of postage and he felt that some co-ordination could be made between the various committees and the Secretary, and that all bulletins should be passed through the Secretary to ensure that bulletins were not sent round unnecessarily. It was not a matter of reducing the number, he said, but rather to ensure that there was some co-ordination, which the Secretary agreed to do.

As far as I can recall the first bulletin I was responsible for was No. 109 of January 1971 which I issued in my then role as assistant secretary. I ended it with the following item:

> OLD HABITS: It was hoped to dye the old nuns' habits from "Bonaventure" for "A Letter from the General" but the attempt was not successful, which only goes to show that old habits dye hard.

Things have not improved on the humour front.

All bulletins now use the standard A4 paper size but we did not use that until No. 135 of 20 June 1973 which was issued by the secretary of the social committee, John Owens. Before that the bulletins had been mainly quarto with the occasional larger ones on foolscap paper. There was a brief lapse (two issues) back into quarto in 1976 and foolscap (also two issues) in 1978 and finally (one issue) in 1982!

To date there have been eight principal editors of the bulletin.

The first two hundred were mainly the work of Peter Tunstill with the odd individual issue by others, principally the social committee or the publicity officer. I produced six issues in late 1980 and early 1981 until Ann Hurlstone, as secretary, took over for the next sixty or so (1981 to 1987), again with individual issues by the social committee or the publicity officer

Judith Robinson did a two year stint from April 1987 to March 1989 and that, or slightly less, became the norm over the next five years with Humphrey Gawthrop in the editor's chair from May 1989 to March 1991, followed by Ann Haycock from May 1991 to March 1993 and Bruce Haycock from April 1993 to September 1994. I became bulletin editor again in November 1994 with issue No. 348 and, with two short breaks (Humphrey Gawthrop three issues in 2001 and Rob Vaughan three issues in 2005-6), I have edited it ever since, but I am still a long way short of Peter Tunstill's twenty years or so record.

The advent of desktop publishing revolutionised the look of the bulletin and the way it is produced. The first time this was used was for No. 346 edited by

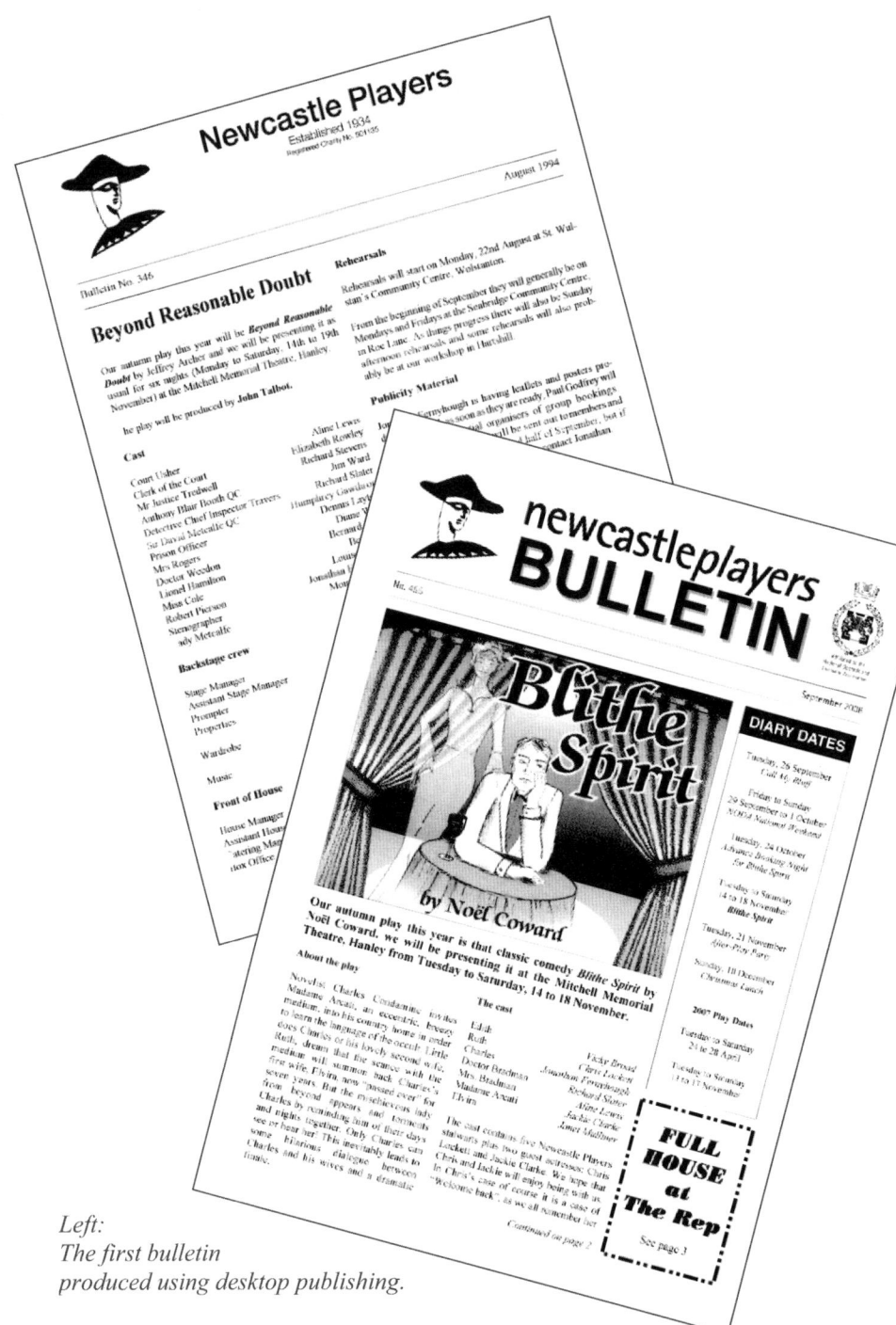

Left:
The first bulletin produced using desktop publishing.

Right:
How the bulletin looks now after twelve years or so of desktop publishing.

Di West and myself in August 1994 while Bruce and Ann Haycock were away for the month. From No. 348 all bulletins have been produced in this way.

Pictures are taken for granted nowadays, but the first, drawn by hand, appeared in an unnumbered and undated bulletin issued by the social committee in September 1964. The artist was Enid Tunstill and there was a note beneath it, typical of Enid:

> Signed tracings of this masterpiece are obtainable on request.

During Bruce Haycock's editorship drawings and maps became a regular feature, but it was not until May 1995 that there were any photographs. The first were in a reproduction of a *Sentinel* article including pictures of Pat Mason, Alan Davies and Ben Devall. From early 1999 there were photographs in nearly every issue and the July issue that year (No. 396) carried an extensive photographic report of Janet and Rob Vaughan's wedding at the Theatre Royal, Bath. Now, a bulletin without at least one photograph would be very unusual.

The latest innovation – an electronic version of the bulletin – came about as a result of the Royal Mail's new method of charging postage which came into effect on 21st August 2006.

Up to and including issue No. 454 (August 2006) bulletins were sent out to members unfolded in C4 (229 x 324 mm) envelopes. Under the new system these are classed as large letters. We calculated that by folding the bulletin and using the smaller C5 (162 x 229 mm) envelopes we would save in the region of £80 a year in postal charges. As an alternative, though, we offered members the chance to receive the bulletin more quickly (and in colour) by email, a method which we had already been using for a few months to send the bulletin to two members now living in Spain.

Email is also used from time to time to draw members' attention to special events. Unfortunately there are still quite a lot of members who do not have access to email, so the bulletin, sent by post, remains the major channel of communication with our members.

Communicating with our patrons

We have a patrons mailing list for many years and we use this as a way of publicising our productions to potential ticket buyers. For a long time this was

Newcastle Players NEWS

March 2000

Dear Theatregoer,

This issue of *Newcastle Players News* contains information about:

- ☑ our next production.
- ☑ changes in our performance days in May
- ☑ new ticket booking facilities
- ☑ our November production.

Newcastle Players NEWS

August 2000

Affiliated to the National Operatic and Dramatic Association

Mitchell Memorial Theatre Open Day
Saturday 12th August 2000

The Newcastle Players will be one of a number of groups taking part in a special Open Day at the Mitchell Memorial Theatre between 12 noon and 4 p.m. on Saturday 12th August 2000.

It will be presented at the Mitchell Memorial Theatre, Hanley from Tuesday to Saturday, 14th to 18th November 2000.

For technical reasons there will be no public performance on Monday 13th November but there will be a matinee on Saturday 18th November. Tickets for the matinee will be at a reduced price.

Booking details will be sent to you later next month, but in the meantime please make a note of the dates in your diary.

Help the Newcastle Players to help Children in Need

Newcastle Players NEWS

March 2002

Affiliated to the National Operatic and Dramatic Association

Sad loss of Ben Devall an…

Newcastle Players have been saddened over the pa… respected and stalwart members: Ben Devall, our P… last year and Mary Blakeman, a notable figurehe… died at the end of December 2000…

newcastleplayers
Established 1934
Registered Charity No. 501135
NEWS

March 2004

For more information telephone 01782 627551 Publicity

Affiliated to the National Operatic and Dramatic Association

2004 is a Celebration Year for Newcastle Players –

In November, it will be 70 … society was founded…

Special One Off Offer

In order to welcome any new clubs or societies to our block booking facilities, we are making a **very special introductory offer when they book 10 tickets or more.** If you belong to a society whom you think would like to take advantage of this offer, please contact the Ticket Secretary on 01782 617055.

Recent Plays

…ce our last Newsletter in 2002 we have …formed 3 very varied plays. Those of you … came to see the Exorcism by Don Taylor … many appreciative comments to us. It … exciting production and called upon … performances from the four …ers.

newcastleplayers
Established 1934
Registered Charity No. 501135
NEWS

Affiliated to the National Operatic and Dramatic Association

September 2004 — For more information telephone 01782 627551 Publicity

70th Anniversary Celebrations –

Our special year is continuing with the hilarious farce 'It Runs in the Family' by Ray Cooney and we will be publishing a special souvenir programme for the event.

This very popular production is guaranteed to have you in stitches - rather appropriately it is set in a hospital, the Doctors common room at St Andrews Hospital.

It follows the hilarious plight of neurology specialist, Dr. David Mortimer who whilst preparing for the most important lecture of his life, is confronted by the consequences of a youthful amorous adventure. The humour created by his ever more frantic explanations is further confused by fellow doctors preparing for the Christmas panto, a wandering senile patient and an assortment of matrons, real or otherwise.

It will be performed at the Mitchell Memorial Theatre from Tuesday November 9th to Saturday 13th November 2004 at 7.30 and there is a matinee at 3.00 p.m. on Saturday 13th. Full details are given on the enclosed leaflet.

Charity Donation

This November we will be making a charitable donation to the Donna Louise Trust during the run of the play, as, unlike previous years the production does not coincide with BBC Children in Need appeal. We will be taking a collection for the Trust during the week and also making a donation from our …

Discount Offer to Groups

We are once again offering a cut price reduction of 50% to **NEW** group bookings of 10 or more. If you belong to a society who would like to take advantage of this offer for the first time, please contact the Ticket …

newcastleplayers
Established 1934
Registered Charity No. 501135
NEWS

Affiliated to the National Operatic and Dramatic Association

February 2005 — For more information telephone 01782 627551 Publicity

70TH Anniversary Celebrations

To conclude our year of celebration this spring the Newcastle Players are putting on a cracking thriller "The Ghost Train" by Arnold Ridley.

"Ghostly goings on" and "murderous mysteries" abound as a group of train passengers are stranded for the night at Fal Vale station. Set in the roaring Twenties, this thriller will have you on the edge of your seat, as you try and decide if the strange events and tales of rail disasters are the work of "spooks" or are other forces at work.

Although the Newcastle Players were founded in 1934 our first production was in the spring of 1935 and "The Ghost Train was the play that launched the players 70 years ago. So this is quite an historic re-run. It will be performed from Tuesday 12th April to Saturday 16th April 2005 at 7.30pm. There is also a matinee on Saturday 16th April at 3.00pm at "the Mitchell Memorial Theatre".

About the Author continued

Arnold throughout his life enjoyed playing cricket and rugby and was president of Bath Rugby Club in the 1950's. Arnold played 'Saul Hodgkin the stationmaster' in 1962 at the Yvonne Arnaud Theatre in Guilford His other work included roles in 'The Archers', 'Crossroads' and 'Coronation Street'. In 1967 he was cast as Private Godfrey in *Dad's Army* and by 1968 he was a household name. After 'Dad's Army', Arnold was awarded an OBE for services to the theatre in the Queen's New Year's Honours List of 1982. Unfortunately at the time, failing health was overtaking Arnold, and his lively imagination died along with him in 1984 at the age of 88.

Website

You can now look up our website to keep up to date with Newcastle Players happenings.

The address is http://newcastleplayers.org.uk

done simply by sending out a leaflet and booking form to everyone on the list. Then a few years ago we started to send out a patron's newsletter (*Newcastle Players NEWS*) as well, giving not only details of the next production but also more general information about the society. This is in the form of a single A4 sheet, generally printed on one side only, but sometimes stretching to a second side.

Communicating with the public at large

In 2004 we embraced the electronic age with our own website which can be accessed at www.newcastleplayers.org.uk. It contains a brief history of the society and what we do, news about our current activities, information about forthcoming productions, details of past productions with photographs of the more recent ones, details of how to join the society, a facility for contacting us and links to related websites.

Typing "Newcastle Players" into a Google search will bring up links to thousands of sites relating to footballers who play for Newcastle United, but adding a word such as "theatre" will narrow it down, not to our website, but to the other websites which have links to it such as www.bbc.co.uk/stoke/, www.sgfl.org.uk/mitchell_theatre, www.creativestoke.org.uk/performing.html, www.amdram.co.uk, www.stoke.gov.uk, www.ukwhatsonguide.co.uk//MID Theatres and so on.

Opposite page: examples of Newcastle Players NEWS.

18. Newcastle Players People

The most important asset of any society such as the Newcastle Players is the people who belong to it, its members. When the society started it had three dozen members. Now it is around a hundred and the membership has hovered around that number for quite a few years. However, anybody who takes the trouble to count the different names listed in our programmes over the last seventy or so years will end up with a figure of well over 500. And that is only the people who are mentioned by name. Add all the people who have been or are members but don't get their names in the programme – those who take tickets, show people to their seats, sell programmes, serve drinks in the interval and so on – and the number who have passed through the Newcastle Players could be approaching a thousand.

In writing about Newcastle Players people I faced a problem: if I try to mention everybody, I am bound to cause offence by missing somebody out. I decided, therefore, to list all the current members in an appendix (Appendix C) and, in the main, as far as past members are concerned to limit myself to those whose obituaries have appeared in our programmes and/or our bulletin. The other problem was the order I should follow and here the easiest way out seemed to be alphabetical order by surname.

John Barstow

John Barstow served the Newcastle for nearly forty years occupying important administrative posts in the society for all but the first few months of his membership.

He joined the Newcastle Players in 1939 and in March 1940 he was elected Honorary Secretary. He held that position until becoming Vice President and an Honorary Life Member in 1952. He succeeded John Legge as President in 1963 and occupied that position until his death at the age of 77 in 1977.

John acted in three productions – *Murder on the Second Floor* (April 1939), *Bird in Hand* (January 1940) and *The Blue Goose* (April 1948) – but acting was not his forte. In fact he is reputed to have turned to the audience in one play and announced, "My mind is a complete blank." Perhaps that is why, as

Peter Tunstill wrote in his tribute to the late President, John, while always 'game', was "ever hopeful of getting a good non-speaking part".

John was an outstandingly good President, keenly interested in both people and events in the society and he fulfilled his office with sustained enthusiasm and dedication.

It was his proud boast that he missed attending only one play during his 38 years' membership of the Players.

John Barstow

Dorothy Beardmore

When Dorothy Beardmore joined the Newcastle Players she was no stranger to the stage for she had been a member of the North Staffordshire Amateur Operatic Society for a number of years and appeared in their productions many times. Her debut with us was in a one-act play *(There's Always Spring)* in 1980. She followed that with a very impressive performance as Sister Josephine in *Bonaventure* (1982), imposing great strength of character on the part and giving the type of reliable and proficient performance which we came to take for granted from her.

From then on Dorothy appeared regularly in our productions until

Dorothy Beardmore

illness, which led to her death in June 1993, forced her to withdraw from active participation. She took both comedy and straight drama in her stride. Naturally elegant, she was not averse to letting her hair down for comedy roles which demanded it, as she did in *Cure for Love* (1984). Dorothy's last role for the Newcastle Players was as Mrs Hepworth in *Hobson's Choice* (1991), a part which demanded grace, elegance and strength of character. It could have been tailor-made for her.

As well as treading the boards Dorothy produced one act plays and worked backstage as prompter and wardrobe or properties mistress. She also served on various committees where her down-to-earth common sense was invaluable. In all this Dorothy enjoyed the unfailing support of her husband Eric who continues to play his part as a member of the front-of-house team.

Mary Blakeman

Mary Blakeman, who died in 2000 shortly before her 89th birthday, was responsible for more Newcastle Players productions than anybody else in our history.

Mary was passionate about the theatre from a very early age. Throughout her life she made a point of seeing as many of the stars of the stage as she could and took advantage of opportunities to study under such greats as Alec Guinness and Tyrone Guthrie.

Talking to a *Sentinel* reporter in 1999 she explained that her own acting experience began with a little group called the Five Towns Players in the early forties but, she went on, "It broke up because all the men were called up to fight in the war. The Newcastle Players were still going so I ended up joining them in 1942 and remained with them ever since."

Mary's first appearance in a Newcastle Players production was as Freda in *Nine till Six* at the Marsh Street Assembly Rooms in Newcastle from 23rd to 28th November 1942. She followed that with the part of Mrs. Webb in *Yes and No*, first at Marsh Street (from 22nd to 27th February 1943) and then at the Congregational Church Hall in Chesterton (on 6th and 8th July 1943).

She appeared in several plays after that but it is as a producer that she is best known. That came first about when she was called on to take over a production due to the illness of the our founder and original main producer, John Rowley. Since then she was responsible for over sixty Newcastle Players productions.

But Mary had a much wider commitment to the theatre than just her work for the Newcastle Players. She was a qualified drama adjudicator, a member of the Council of the National Drama Festivals Association, a founder member of the North Staffordshire Drama Association and Chairman of the Stoke-on-Trent Youth and Community Service's Drama Advisory Committee from its inception.

For many years Mary was a trustee of the Victoria Theatre and then the New Victoria Theatre and she worked tirelessly for both. This contribution to the professional theatre locally was recognised in 1992 when she was made an Honorary President of the New Victoria Theatre.

Mary Blakeman

In 1997 her commitment to the Mitchell Memorial Theatre is acknowledged on a plaque above seat P6 unveiled by Dr Gordon Mitchell, son of the aircraft designer Reginald Mitchell after whom the theatre was named. It is dedicated to her "with affection to honour her exemplary voluntary commitment and support since this memorial building appeal was launched in 1943."

Mary's final honour during her lifetime was the award by Keele University of an honorary Master of the University degree in recognition of her services to theatre and drama. The citation rightly described her as "A woman who has become a legend in North Staffordshire theatre circles".Commenting on this in an obituary published in *Amateur Stage* magazine Irene Rostron added:

> Yet Mary's feet, as always, remained firmly on the ground; to her the most important thing remained the future endeavour and success of the theatre in her region. Her example will remain an inspiration and Mary herself a 'legend' to the many who knew and loved her.

A lasting tribute to Mary was made in the form of a video produced by Ray Johnson of Staffordshire University to commemorate her importance to the theatrical life of the Potteries and Newcastle-under-Lyme. Entitled "Mary - A Tribute to Mary Blakeman" it runs for 40 minutes and contains reminiscences by several Newcastle Players members (Enid and Tony Frieder, Ann Haycock, Geoff Price, Buffie Rowley and Jim Ward with other members seen in the background), extracts from the film *Five Towns* which was professionally produced in the forties by the Board of Trade and which Mary appeared in plus Mary's own memories of that episode in her life. Tribute is also paid by Peter Cheeseman and by Stuart Clamp to Mary's contribution to the Victoria Theatre, Hartshill (and its successor the New Victoria Theatre, Basford) and the Mitchell Memorial Theatre respectively. Particularly enjoyable are extracts – featuring Ben Devall and Mary herself – from a video of the party the society arranged for Mary's 80th birthday.

Doug and Edna Challinor

Doug and Edna Challinor joined the society in the early seventies and, until his death in 1980, Doug with Edna's support was active as an actor (*A Lady in a Cage*, *Trap for a Lonely Man*, *The Amorous Prawn* and *Suddenly at Home*), one-act play producer and house manager. If Doug had a fault it was his inability to suppress an urge to add an unrehearsed piece of funny business to his part, much to the discomfiture of fellow actors caught unawares by it.

After Doug's death in 1980 Edna continued to be a dependable member of the front-of-house team and regularly attended the society's social functions until shortly before she moved into a retirement home. She died in January 2004.

The Connelly Family

Denis and Joan Connelly were founder members of the Newcastle Players, Denis playing the part of Richard Winthrop in the original production of *The Ghost Train* and Joan being the prompter. They were later joined in the society by Ceilia Rathbone, who was to become Denis's wife, and later still by Denis and Ceilia's son and daughter, Michael and Anne.

Denis went on to appear in a further thirty-two plays, the last being *The Rape of the Belt* (April 1969). Crippled with arthritis and only able to move with difficulty, he made full use of his resonant voice as Zeus, king of the Gods, a part he was able to play from a seated position, only his face being visible.

As well as being an outstanding actor Denis also worked very hard on the administrative side of the society. He was an accountant by profession and was the society's auditor from 1948 until his death in 1970. Additionally he was Vice-President from 1963, again until his death in 1970. Ironically he was elected a Life Member at the 1970 Annual General Meeting.

Ceilia Connelly (née Rathbone) joined the society in February 1945 and by the following year's Annual General Meeting had become a member of the social committee. She made her Newcastle Players debut in *No Medals* in 1949 and went on to appear in several more plays over the next few years. She was also wardrobe mistress, property mistress or prompter for a number of productions, but it was in the early sixties that she found her true niche, looking after our box office arrangements which she did so well for so long. During that time her son and daughter, Michael and Anne, followed on the family tradition on-stage and backstage before they both moved out of the district.

Ceilia Connelly

She was elected a Life Member in 1978. In acknowledging the honour she said she was proud to receive it and looked upon it as a furtherance of the Connelly tradition. In January 1988, Ceilia suffered a massive stroke and spent most of the last ten years of her life in Madeley Manor Nursing Home where she died in March 1998.

As already mentioned Joan Connelly, or Joan Osborne, as she later became, was one of the original members of the Newcastle Players. In 1935, when she prompted the original production of *The Ghost Train*, she was 17 years old. Over the next twenty years or so she took acting parts in fifteen productions and then subsequently was property mistress on a couple of occasions. In later life she was a regular member of the front-of-house team.

Joan also served on various committees during her seventy years' membership of the society and in her early twenties was Treasurer for a period. In later years, until ill health restricted her activities, she remained a loyal member of the front-of-house team and could generally be found 'beyond the hatch' in the foyer of The Mitchell Memorial Theatre, greeting our patrons and manning the cloakroom.

Alan Davies

Alan Davies was a member of the Newcastle Players for over twenty years. He joined the society with his wife Margaret in 1977 and was the type of stalwart essential for the success of a society such as ours. His contribution did not usually attract the limelight, although he did appear in two plays, in a non-speaking role on each occasion. The first time was in *Murder in Mind* in November 1990. He took a bow at the end of the performance but received no credit in the programme, not out of disrespect for Alan but to heighten the mystery of the play, since he played a corpse, so it was not only a non-speaking role but a non-living one. On the second occasion (in *Two into One* in April 1996) his appearance with his wife Margaret as a hotel guest was duly acknowledged.

Alan was, however, usually more at home doing many of the jobs in the society which are out of the glare of the stage lights but no less essential to a successful production. He contributed many hours of hard work at our workshop helping to build sets; he was a regular member of our front of house team and served for a number of years on several of our key committees. He died in September 1999.

Ben Devall

Alfred George Devall, his official name, was known to everybody as Ben. He joined the Newcastle Players in 1947 and during the first fifteen years of his membership he appeared on stage in ten plays. It could be said that there was something seasonal about his acting career. It started with *Winter Sunshine* and *Autumn*, both in 1947, and was followed a few years later by *Breath of Spring*. He modestly referred to his "small parts" and in fact the characters often did not even have a name. In *No Medals* for example he was the sentry, in *Viceroy Sarah* a footman, in *Witness for the Prosecution* the court usher and in *You Can't Take It With You* simply a man. Small as Ben's parts may have been, they were not unimportant and his dependability in such parts became a byword in the Newcastle Players. It is perhaps worth mentioning that between *Winter Sunshine* (1947) and *You Can't Take It With You* (1962) 105 actors and actresses took the stage in our productions and 95 of them appeared in fewer plays than Ben did.

Over the years Ben served on various committees. For eight or nine years he was secretary of the social committee; from 1975 to 1985 he was treasurer; he was one of the hardest working members of our front of house team and was House Manager or Assistant House Manager on several occasions during the seventies. Later on, as President, he loved attending to the VIPs in the hospitality room, though he did confess once that he had found one the Mayors rather hard going. "I couldn't get him to open his mouth, except to empty his glass," said Ben, a fact which he probably recorded in one of the many ditties for which we remember him.

Ben Devall

But without doubt Ben's most memorable service was his work on our sets, particularly the backcloths. He was a gifted watercolour painter and for many years he devoted his artistic talents to painting a new backcloth for every one of our productions. To suit the location of the play his subjects were as varied as a tropical island, a country village cricket pitch or a street in a northern town. For *A Friend Indeed* it was the Rome skyline.

After reading the play Ben often did a pen and ink sketch before producing a small watercolour to the same proportions as the finished backcloth. Then he got down to the full-scale job. The backcloth could be as big as twenty feet wide by fourteen feet high, although each member of the audience would only see a small part of that. And only the cast and backstage team – if they knew where to look – would see the cheeky little figures that Ben used to delight in painting in an obscure spot on the backcloth.

Ben was made a Life Member in 1987 and elected President in 1990 a very fitting mark of recognition of his many years of unstinting service. His wife Margaret was made a Life Member in 2005.

Humphrey Gawthrop

Humphrey Gawthrop joined the society in 1986 after moving to the north of the county from Stafford where he had been in practice as a solicitor. He also worked for a time as a solicitor in Audley but retired early following heart trouble. However, a successful heart bypass operation appeared to have put him back on his feet and, although he resigned from the Newcastle Players a couple of years before his death in January 2004, he continued to perform on the musical stage.

Humphrey was a person it was not easy to overlook. He had an imposing presence which he put to good use from his very first appearance on stage for the society as Waldo Lydecker in *Laura* (986). He followed this with parts in a further twenty-one full-length or one-act plays over a period of fifteen years. He also produced eight plays ranging from the one-acter *Dark Brown* in July 1987 to *Straight & Narrow* in April/May 1999. He also worked as a member of the backstage crew and was in fact an outstanding prompter. As one member commented, "Humphrey seemed to sense – almost before the actor did – that a prompt was needed and he always gave it clearly and without hesitation". Offstage he served on several of the society's committees at various times and he was the society's secretary in 1989 and 1990.

Humphrey Gawthrop

Paul Godfrey

Paul Godfrey joined the Newcastle Players in 1967 and, like most members at the time, he made his acting debut in a one-act play: *This Desirable Cottage* in September of that year. The first full-length play he appeared in was *Dear Charles* the following year. He made his directing debut with a one-act play, *The Invisible Worm,* in July 1971. Then, after combining acting and directing for a time, he decided to concentrate on direction and over a period of twenty-eight years he directed a total of fourteen full-length plays for us.

Paul was a demanding but courteous director and a joy to work with. He expected his cast to give of their best, but recognised the limitations some had, coupled with the wisdom not to expect the impossible. Here are just a few of the many tributes paid to him when he died in 2005 :

> There are good and bad producers or, should I say, easy and difficult ones; Paul was one of the former, always comfortable to work with even when stresses and strains, as they do, arose. (Di West)
>
> It was always a pleasure to work with Paul either on-stage or Front of House; his dry wit and easy-going manner made appearing in a play he was directing an absolute pleasure. (Richard Slater)

Paul Godfrey

> Paul performed in many one-act plays and other major productions, eventually moving on to producing a number of our plays, which he did with skill, understanding and great humour. (Buffie Rowley)

As well as directing (or producing as it was originally called) Paul carried out many other duties both backstage and front-of-house, including Stage Manager and House Manager. He was the society's Vice-Chairman from 1984 to 1987, Chairman from 1987 to 1990 and Treasurer from 1990 to 1993.

John Legge

John Legge was Vice-Chairman of the Newcastle Players for a few months in 1946 and was elected Chairman in August of that year following the resignation of Ernest Butterworth. He continued as Chairman until 1952 when the title of the post was changed to President. He continued in that office until his death at the age of 82 in February 1963.

When John Legge became our Chairman he was still the Borough Treasurer for Newcastle, although he retired from the position, which he had held for 29 years, the following year.

In a tribute published in Bulletin No. 42 dated 14th March, 1963 Peter Tunstill wrote:

> John was perhaps the most enthusiastic President we have had; the interest he took in the activities of the society and the effort he put into everything he tackled on our behalf will be remembered by all those who had the privilege of serving under him.

The Mason Family

Jack and Eluned Mason were involved in the Newcastle Players from the very beginning. Jack was one of the founders with John Rowley in 1934 and he was the society's Chairman from then until December 1938 owing to ill health, at which point he was elected our first Life Member. He returned to office as Vice-Chairman in 1943 and occupied that post until his death in 1945.

Although Eluned Mason's connections with the society, like Jack's, went back to the very beginning in 1934, she was not officially accepted as a member until the rule excluding non-Catholics was removed. That she was involved from the start, member or not, is beyond dispute as her signature on a copy of the programme for our 1935 production of *The Ghost Train* clearly proves.

Eluned Mason

From 1936 onwards her name was rarely out of our programmes: first as costume mistress, which later developed into costumes and properties (she even had to do sound effects on at least one occasion), then as an actress and latterly as a Life Member. She also served on many committees and, when not acting or working backstage, she was to be seen helping out front of house: selling programmes, taking tickets or serving refreshments.

Eluned's first acting part was as Miss Snell in *Murder on the Second Floor* at the Marsh Street Assembly Rooms, Newcastle in April 1939 and her last was a brief but telling appearance as Mrs Blacken in the one-act play *Careful Rapture* at the Mitchell Memorial Theatre in July 1980.

Over this period of forty years or so Eluned was seen in a variety of roles. In November 1952, for example, she played Anne, Queen of England, in *Viceroy Sarah* at the Municipal Hall, Newcastle. Of her acting in that part the *Evening Sentinel* said she "gave a most finished study, playing with an ease and sincerity which was most convincing".

Due to failing health Eluned was unable to see our production of *Laura* in April 1986, but she remained as keenly interested as ever and she insisted on being provided with a copy of the script so that she could see what she was missing. She died two weeks before our November production that year.

Jack and Eluned's son Pat and his wife Janet have also been members of the Newcastle Players for many years. Pat's first recollections of the society are being allowed to put the cushions out on the seats as a small boy. As he put it many years later, "I suppose it was easier, rather than get a sitter-in, to take Pat along as well." On one occasion it went further than that, for Pat and his sister Barbara appeared as small children in our production of *Quality Street* in 1936.

After World War II Barbara and her husband Peter Carryer emigrated to Canada but Pat became, like his parents, a stalwart of the society, which was recognised in 1992 when he was awarded life membership.

The Rowley Family

The following is a slightly edited version of a tribute to John Rowley by Mary Blakeman which appeared in the programme for our Golden Jubilee production of *Outside Edge* in 1984:

> It was John Rowley's love of the theatre and his not inconsiderable talent for acting that inspired him, along with a few fellow enthusiasts, to found the amateur dramatic society which eventually became the Newcastle Players. From the onset he also displayed a great interest in and aptitude for producing plays. He had the ability to evoke the very best from his actors and was adept at encouraging and guiding the less experienced ones.
>
> It is probably true to say that, after his family, the Newcastle Players was John's main interest in life and he gave to it unstintingly of his time and expertise even after his health began to fail. His untimely death at the

age of forty-six was a sad loss to the local amateur stage. Happily, however, his family have continued their association with the society.

The fact that the Newcastle Players continue to flourish is undoubtedly the best tribute that can be paid to John Rowley. He gave the society a firm foundation, always exacting a high standard of performance from its members both on stage and backstage. Those who have been privileged to follow in his footsteps will forever hold him in grateful and happy remembrance.

John's wife Jo, who outlived him by fifty-five years, was born in Dublin and came to England at the age of fourteen with her brothers who were all younger. In 1932 she married John Rowley and moved to Newcastle. In the society's early years Jo appeared in two plays – as Arabel Moulton-Barrett in *The Barretts of Wimpole Street* (1935) and Harriet Carroll in *The Two Mrs. Carrolls* (1937) – but her duties to her family prevented her from playing a more active part, at first as John was heavily committed to the society as its producer and also as an actor, but later during his long illness and then during the difficult times following his early death.

John Rowley

Two of John and Jo's daughters – Buffie and Annie – continue the Rowley family's connection with the Newcastle Players, Buffie – actually her official name is Elizabeth – once said that, as her parents were so involved in Newcastle Players, her life grew around the society. It is, therefore, quite fitting that she should be a Life Member and our current President.

Bill Stevens

Bill Stevens and his wife Vida joined the Newcastle Players in July 1938. Bill immediately became a member of the backstage team and in November of that year he was Assistant Stage Manager for *The Wind and the Rain*. In the next production (*Murder on the Second Floor* in April 1939) Bill made his first and last acting appearance playing the parts of 2nd Police Constable and The Man with the Box. He also became Stage Manager. In fact he stage-managed every other Newcastle Players production for the next twenty years, some 37 plays in all.

Agatha Christie's *Witness for the Prosecution* (November 1959) may have been the last play Bill stage-managed, but it was by no means an end to his interest in what went on backstage. Every stage manager from then until his death in 1990 benefited from Bill's encouragement and advice, and he continued to design our sets and supervise their construction for many years.

Bill Stevens

For many people a contribution such as Bill made to the backstage activities of our society would have been enough. But not for him. Whether at committee meetings, social functions, set building sessions at our Hartshill workshop or, most important of all, our performances in the theatre, Bill could always be counted on to be present.

He was an officer of the society for thirty years: Treasurer from 1961 to 1971; Vice-President from 1970 to 1977; and President from 1977 until 1990. However, the office of President changed during Bill's tenure. When Bill was first elected to the post the President ran the society – albeit with the help of the executive committee. In 1984 Bill signified that he would like to be relieved of this heavy responsibility. The society agreed but, in gratitude for Bill's services, asked him to stay on as President and created the new office of Chairman to take over the executive functions.

Many tributes were paid to Bill after his death. One was by Ben Devall, who succeeded him as President. Ben wrote:

> That there is no record of Bill acting again after April 1939 serves to underline the fact that membership of an amateur dramatic society does not necessarily go hand in hand with acting. Many members prefer to

get stuck in with the practicalities, hammering out the problems of a set, hammering the set together, teaching new members how it's done – Bill was one of these. He acquired a vast experience and constantly passed it on.

Bill's wife Vida was made a Life Member in 1989. Their son and daughter, Richard an Judith, were both active in the society but now live out of the district, Richard in fact in Spain.

John Talbot

For well over forty years John Talbot made an enormous contribution to the success of the Newcastle Players through a long list of polished performances, both as an actor and as a producer. And when not directly involved in a production he would pull his weight as a member of the front-of-house team.

John's stage career began at the age of four when he appeared in an infants school production of *Peter Pan*. But his interest in the theatre really got under way at Wolstanton County Grammar School in his teens under the eagle eye of Ernest Kershaw, a major figure in the history of amateur drama in North Staffordshire. He also appeared in Youth Club productions in Newcastle and then National Service called. During that period he only managed to fit in a single one-act play. On leaving the army he joined the Triginta Modern Players and also acted with the Stoke-on-Trent Shakespearean Society before becoming a member of the Newcastle Players in 1953.

John Talbot

The Hollow by Agatha Christie (November 1953) was the first Newcastle Players production John appeared in. He played the part of Edward Angkatell but, when asked about it many years later, he admitted that he could not remember it very well. Not surprising seeing that he acted in nearly fifty major productions for the society and produced a further ten. John's last appearance on stage for the Newcastle Players was in Patrick Cargill's comedy *Don't*

Misunderstand Me (April 1995) where he and Bob West created, in the words of John Fox of *The Sentinel*, "a splendid double act, showing exceptional talent in dealing with the complicated stories they have to fabricate." His last production for the society was Ray Cooney's *Two Into One* in April 1996. Ironically his last role on stage was not with the Newcastle Players but making a guest appearance in the North Staffordshire Amateur Operatic Society's production of *Carousel* at the Queen's Theatre, Burslem in October 1996 less than a year before he died.

Peter Tunstill

Peter Tunstill joined the Newcastle Players in the early 1940s. The exact date is shrouded in some mystery for, while he definitely played the part of Hugh Randolph in *Dear Octopus* in November 1941, his membership was not confirmed until January 1942.

Other plays Peter appeared in were *Another Language* (1944), *Hawk Island* (1944), *Winter Sunshine* (1947), *Autumn* (1947), *No Medals* (1949) and *Viceroy Sarah* (1952). As late as July 1975 he even appeared in the one-acter *Afternoon at the Seaside* by Agatha Christie.

Peter Tunstill

However, it was in an administrative capacity that Peter made his main contribution to the success of the Newcastle Players. And it was an enormous contribution. Many of today's members who knew Peter probably assume that he had always been an officer of the society or, at least, a member of the Executive Committee, but that was not so. He was was first co-opted to the committee in 1949 "as publicity man for the next production". At the committee's April 1955 meeting he was appointed Publicity Manager for the ensuing 12 months and the minutes record that he "should be invited to the executive meetings where publicity was involved."

He became the society's secretary in 1958 and occupied that post until 1981. Even after ill health forced him to relinquish it he continued to serve, first for a brief period as public relations officer and then, until shortly before his death in 1989, as advertising manager.

We often say that the actors the audience sees are only the tip of the theatrical iceberg. It is usual to go on to mention the backstage crew, the scenery builders, the programme sellers, stewards and other members of the front of house staff. It is true that Peter was seldom absent from the foyer or auditorium during the run of a play. He was in fact House Manager for many of our productions. But his contribution was not confined to the two weeks or so each year that we perform at the Mitchell Memorial Theatre. He rarely missed either the society's social functions or meetings of any committee that he was appointed to.

In fact Peter's work for the Newcastle Players was almost unceasing, much of it, for all of his excellence as a front man, unseen by the public at large. His activities out of the limelight helped to oil the bearings of our organisation and make everything run smoothly. And it was in recognition of these services that he was made a Life Member of the society in 1978.

Peter Tunstill was one of the central figures of the society for many years and it is perhaps fitting that he should bring this chapter about Newcastle Players people to a close. Peter was very much a Newcastle Players person.

19. From Amateur to Professional

Many professional actors started in the amateur ranks. Others, while making the occasional foray into the professional world, remain committed to the amateur theatre. Four Newcastle Players members in this category that come to mind are Mary Blakeman, Ann McArdle, Jonathan Fernyhough and James Lawton.

In 1947 the Central Office of Information produced a documentary film about the pottery industry. It was entitled *The Five Towns* and had its premiere at the Capitol cinema in Hanley the following year. The production crew was professional as was one member of the cast, an actress playing a visitor to Stoke-on-Trent from 'down south'. All the other actors and actresses were local amateurs, one of whom was Mary Blakeman. They were paid £3 a day.

Ann McArdle has been treading the amateur boards since she was a teenager, with the Newcastle Players and with local operatic societies too. But, without compromising her amateur status in any way, she has also been seen on the television screen in a professional capacity in a number of series including *Doctors, The Forsyte Saga* and *Stretford Wives* to name but three.

Jonathan Fernyhough is also involved in the musical theatre as well as the Newcastle Players. From the beginning of 2002 to December 2003 he and Becky Bonell presented a Sunday afternoon show on BBC Radio Stoke called *Becky & Jonathan,*. This gave Jonathan the opportunity to interview a number of well-known people such as Lord Attenborough, Joan Collins, Christopher Biggins and Dec Cluskey. He is hopeful of doing more radio work in the future.

James Lawton appeared in a number of musicals put on by the Porthill Players before he joined the Newcastle Players and switched to straight acting. As with other members his first commitment is to his family, his 'day job' and of course the Newcastle Players, but he has signed up with a casting agency and from time to time plays small parts in television commercials and corporate videos.

Then there are those former members who have taken the plunge and entered the professional entertainment world completely.

Harry Oakes

The first Newcastle Players member to turn professional was Harry Oakes, and that was as a radio actor. Originally a pottery designer by profession. Harry had a rich baritone voice and put it to good use in choral singing and musicals. As a member of the Newcastle Players he appeared in our productions of *Distinguished Gathering* (November 1937) and *Bird in Hand* (April 1938), playing Sir Brian Howet and Thomas Greenleaf respectively.

Harry Oakes (left) with other members of "The Archers" cast of 1951 – Bob Arnold (Tom Forrest) and Gwen Berryman (Doris Archer).

Bird in Hand is set in a charming rural setting – a Gloucestershire inn and Greenleaf is the innkeeper A contemporary press review said of the Harry Oakes in that part:

> It would be difficult to imagine a more satisfactory characterisation than that of Mr Harry Oakes in the part of Greenleaf. His performance was sincere and beautifully moving, without a false note from start to finish. This was one of the best studies I have seen on an amateur stage.

During the war, when many of the pottery manufacturers had to close down, Harry went to work for the Ministry of Supply in Birmingham, where he took advantage of opportunities to work in broadcasting. He started off in *Children's Hour* and then graduated to drama and features. This in turn led to him being cast as the original Dan Archer when the long-running radio serial *The Archers* first went on air in the early 1950s, staying with the programme until his death ten years later.

Godfrey Baseley, the original producer of *The Archers,* wrote of Harry Oakes:

> Harry was a warm and friendly person with a ready wit, a sense of fun and above all a great sincerity and attention to detail in all he undertook. These natural qualities were just what we wanted for the character of Dan Archer.

Hilary Tindall

Hilary Tindall joined the Newcastle Players in January 1955 as a girl of eighteen. She appeared in one play – *Down Came a Blackbird* in March of that year – before going on to drama college in London. The *Weekly Sentinel*'s reviewer described her performance as "commendable". Another member of the cast put it better with the comment: "it was obvious that she had talent".

Hilary Tindall was born in Manchester but the family moved to North Staffordshire when her father became manager of The Wheatsheaf Hotel in Stoke. After studying at RADA her initial professional experience was in rep. She made her West End debut in 1960 at the Arts Theatre in *A Trip to the Castle*. Over the next ten years or so she played a wide range of small roles in the theatre. Then in 1972 she got her break when she was cast as the glamorous but treacherous wife, Ann Hammond, in the BBC's drama series *The Brothers* which ran until 1976. Although she loved playing 'scheming bitches', after completing *The Brothers* she spent two years on stage trying to shake off the stigma of Ann Hammond.

Hilary Tindall in "Down Came a Blackbird".

In spite of the success of *The Brothers* Hilary Tindall never achieved international stardom, although she did have a brief period of success in Sweden in the late seventies as a result of appearing in a television series there which was filmed in both English and Swedish.

After acting in a number of situation comedies she accepted another femme fatale role in 1980 in *Tales of the Unexpected* when she played opposite Anthony Valentine. One of her last roles was in the ITV serialisation of Stan Barstow's *A Kind of Loving* in 1982 when she played a bored housewife who seduces one of her husband's employees.

She died of cancer in December 1992.

Geoffrey Saunders

Geoffrey Saunders joined the Newcastle Players in 1962. He played the part of Alphonse in *All for Mary* (November 1964) and was due to play Blandinet in *Don't Listen Ladies!* the following May. Part way through rehearsals though he went down with chickenpox and had to withdraw. He was in charge of music for The *Irregular Verb To Love* (December 1965) which was rather appropriate in view of his subsequent career.

From 1968 to 1971 Geoffrey studied singing at the Royal Manchester College of Music after which he began his professional career with performances in a succession of West End musicals including *Applause* with Lauren Bacall and *Cockie* with Max Wall. He appeared with Sammy Cahn in *Sammy Cahn's Song Book* at Drury Lane, with Sally Anne Howes and Tommy Steele in the first performance of *Hans Anderson* at the London Palladium where he was also Assistant Director. This led to work in regional theatre as Musical Director and Choreographer. Performances in straight theatre include roles in *The Merchant of Venice, Blithe Spirit, Crown Matrimonial, Private Lives, Candida* and *The Hollow Crown*.

Geoffrey Saunders

In 1988 Geoffrey joined the staff of the Royal Northern College of Music, as the Royal Manchester College of Music was now known, as senior tutor in the Opera Department, concentrating on performance techniques. A year later he produced a double bill including Stravinsky's *The Soldier's Tale* at the Cheltenham International Music Festival and in 1993 directed Britten's *A Midsummer Night's Dream* for the RNCM. In February 1996 television and film producer June Howson invited him to choreograph and play the male lead in her stage production of *Stepping Out*.

Since the early 1990's Geoffrey has enjoyed an association with Clonter Opera in Cheshire, where he has directed many opera galas, operettas and operas.

Simon Thompson

Simon Thompson joined the Newcastle Players in April 1985 as a result of a recruiting drive we staged that spring. In July of that year he played Jem Mayston in the one-act play *The Copper Kettle* and in the autumn he was hard at work as a member of our workshop team building the set for *Relative Values* (November 1985). He returned to the acting ranks as Danny Dorgan, the jazz-loving Juilliard School music student, in *Laura* (April-May 1986). In July 1986 he was Albert Smith in another one-acter, *Queer Street*.

Simon Thompson (left) with Mark Kirkham working on the set for "Relative Values in 1985

From 1986 to 1989 Simon studied at the East 15 Acting School in Essex which grew out of the work of John Littlewood's Theatre Work in Stratford East. On graduation he appeared in television productions such as *Prime Suspect*. For three years he acted in Theatre in Education back in North Staffordshire but also in Scotland and the West Country. He has acted in weekly rep, including a season for Charles Vance, publishing editor of *Amateur Stage*, and three summer seasons at the Sheringham Little Theatre in Norfolk where he met his wife Debbie. Other work included a year at the Globe Children's Theatre and a number of corporate videos, including one for Virgin Atlantic. The professional name he used for this work was Richard Hannah, as Equity already had a Simon Thompson on its books.

When acting work dried up Simon and Debbie moved from London back to Norfolk and, after working in a bookshop for three years, he enrolled on the Graduate Teacher Programme, a programme of on-the-job training which allowed him to qualify as a teacher while working. He is now on the staff of Paston Sixth Form College at North Walsham in Norfolk, where he teaches Performance, Acting, Music, Dance and Drama.

In his spare time, Simon also helps out at the Sheringham Little Theatre where Debbie is now artistic director, so the wheel has come full circle.

Paul Wood

In the late eighties and early nineties Paul Wood appeared in a string of Newcastle Players productions. In *Harlequinade* by Terence Rattigan he played the '1st Halberdier'. So he can claim to have been the proverbial spear-carrier at one time.

Paul also acted with several other groups ("Never in musicals", he adds) such as Mow Cop Players, The Rep and New Peoples Theatre. But it was through his work with a friend in a variety act that he earned his Equity card which enabled him to act professionally. He insists that he was really "a dedicated amateur and only a professional with a very small p". Nevertheless he spent some time touring schools with a Theatre in Education company.

Paul Wood

As well as performing Paul worked for ten years as a volunteer at the Theatre Royal in Hanley and then, in 1993, he became the stage door keeper there, staying, through a succession of owners, until the theatre closed in 2000. After a short break he joined the staff of the Regent Theatre and Victoria Hall, where he is now Stage Door Receptionist.

In a *Sentinel Sunday* article Paul was quoted as saying: "Naturally we see many stars but I can say I hardly ever get star-struck." He does, however, admire Nigel Havers as a star of cinema and television who is equally at home performing to the Regent's vast auditorium and he quotes as his favourite comedian Lee Evans, quickly adding "and of course the inevitable Mr Dodd".

Paul says that he was lucky to have been able to perform in Newcastle Players productions alongside such people as John Talbot, Ann McArdle and Bob West. "Particularly John", he says. "He had such a wealth of talent and experience, and I feel privileged that he was prepared to share that with me. He was an inspiration. I am just sorry that I never had the opportunity to get to know him better."

Tom Farrington

Tom Farrington joined the society during the summer of 1992 and immediately got involved as a member of the backstage crew for *Plays for a Summer Evening*, our evening – or three evenings to be more accurate – of one-act plays. He was then involved in most of our productions over the next five years as stage manager (*A Novel Inclination*), assistant stage manager, music and sound effects, or as a member of the set building team and stage crew.

Tom Farrington

When Tom joined us he was training to be an accountant, but in 1995 he abandoned this career path and spent the next two years at Oldham College where in 1997 he gained an HND in Lighting and Sound Design (Electrical Engineering). While at the college he was involved in a variety of productions at its theatre, the Grange Arts Centre, and other theatres, notably the Palace and Opera House, in the Manchester area.

During the 1998 and 1999 summer seasons Tom was stage manager for the show *Mystique* at Blackpool Pleasure Beach. This involved running the show, managing the cast and crew, pyrotechnics, health & safety, setting and testing of illusions, props maintenance, animal handling (cats, dogs and snakes), electrical equipment maintenance, rigging and flying.

Since then Tom has worked on the backstage crew of a whole range of shows at theatres all over the country and also at sea since, during the summer of 2001, he was responsible for the technical aspects of the ship's entertainment on the P&O Cruises liner *Oriana*.

He is currently (August 2006) working as a 'casual' at the The Mayflower theatre in Southampton, where he lives, and studying for a Bsc (Hons) in Physical Science. Quite a change from the accountancy that was once going to be his career.

Simon Milward

Simon Milward's Newcastle Players debut was as Colin in *The House by the Lake* – described the *The Sentinel* as "a very plausible rotter". Simon then appeared in another five productions, most recently as Lieut. Hubert Gruber in *'Allo 'Allo* (May 2003).

Shortly after that Simon was accepted as a student at the Oxford School of Drama in Woodstock, Oxford and the executive committee decided to award him that year's Mary Blakeman Bursary (see next chapter). Acknowledging this Simon wrote:

Simon Milward

> Newcastle Players have played a big part towards my decision to go back to studying Drama. If I hadn't been presented with the opportunity to play some challenging roles, offered encouragement and received some kind comments and useful criticism, I don't think I would have written off to any drama schools.

Since graduating in August 2004 Simon has been on various Theatre in Education Tours to Primary and Secondary schools across the UK dealing with issues such as bullying and 'stranger danger' awareness.

In September 2005 he moved to Dorset where he has worked as a Care Support Worker for adults with learning disabilities at a residential home and also at a local Day Centre teaching adults with learning disabilities on an acting project. In 2006 he enrolled on a teaching course at Salisbury College with a view to teaching drama and running workshops.

Simon's stage credits include *Bullies' Paradise* (Firehouse Touring Theatre), *Merry Olde England* and *Bully 4 You* (Black Cat Touring Theatre), *The Long Goodbye* (Cockpit Theatre, London), *Suddenly Last Summer*, *Ted and Sylvia*, *Trojan Women* and *Hamlet* (The Studios, Oxford) and *A Midsummer Night's Dream* (Pegasus Theatre, Oxford). He has also appeared in the film *Space Cadet* (Carlton TV) and on television in *Doctors* (BBC1) and *30 Minutes* (Carlton TV).

20. Charity Ends Up At Home

The Newcastle Players became a registered charity (No. 501135) in 1971, but that did not and has not stopped us assisting other charitable organisations. Mention has already been made in Chapter 4 of performances staged in the thirties and forties in aid of various charities and in Chapter 5 of our participation in The Royal British Legion's Festival of Remembrance in 1995 plus our donation of £1000 a couple of years before that to The Rep's new theatre building fund.

But there have been other instances of donations to various charitable organisations over the years.

For example, in 1960, which was World Refugee Year, the society decided to give the whole of the proceeds of the Tuesday, March 15th performance of *Breath of Spring* to the Ockenden Venture, an organization originally set up to bring a small group of Latvian and Polish girls from displaced persons camps for education at Ockenden, a country house on the outskirts of Woking. The scheme was subsequently extended to bring displaced people from other countries to the UK for education, training and settlement and a network of centres was built up around the country. The *Breath of Spring* programme contained the following note:

> It is perhaps fitting in this year of the Stoke-on-Trent Jubilee Celebrations and the Newcastle Players 25th Anniversary of their first public performance that they can make some contribution towards the happiness and welfare of those less fortunate than themselves.

Between 1995 and 2000 the Newcastle Players helped Stoke-on-Trent Rotary Club to stage a *Festival of Music* for local schools at the Mitchell Memorial Theatre. This involved a large number of our members led by Paul Godfrey as Front-of-House Manager and John Hough as Stage Manager plus Rotary Club members and several hundred schoolchildren. It was supposed to be a way of helping Rotary in its charitable work but, to our embarrassment, the club insisted in making a donation to our funds.

In 2000 the climax of the BBC's Children in Need Appeal coincided with the Friday performance of our production of *The Importance of Being Earnest* and

Chairman Jim Ward (left), President Elizabeth Rowley and Vice-Chairman Robert Vaughan oresenting a cheque for £500 to Breath of Life Chairman David Lovatt (second right) in November 2005.

we decided to donate part of the proceeds from that performance to the BBC appeal – a decision that paid off. It started with a promise to donate £1 for every ticket sold for the Friday evening because that was when the BBC was staging its own telethon. To this we also added the £100 donation we received from the Rotary Club that year and we appealed to members, patrons and others to add their donations. The Mayor of Newcastle for example sent a cheque from her charity fund. On top of this, a bucket collection was held on the Friday and the audience, the cast, the backstage crew – in fact everybody in the theatre that night – were all persuaded to hand over cash. There was also a smaller leaving collection at the end of the Saturday evening performance. From whatever source the final amount we paid into the BBC Children in Need Appeal account in 2000 was £670.

BBC Children in Need was our chosen charity in each of the following three years. Since then we have chosen charities based closer to home: The Donna Louise Trust (2004 and 2006) and Breath of Life (2005). As our November 2004 production (*It Runs in the Family*) was the first of our Seventieth

Anniversary Year we started off by pledging that we would make a contribution to the Donna Louise Trust – from collections or from our own funds – of at least £70 per performance of. In fact we collected £562.72 so the Executive Committee decided to round this up to £700 – a more appropriate figure for our 70th Anniversary.

And there are also occasions when we make contributions within our own ranks. After Mary Blakeman died in December 2000 we set up an annual bursary worth £150 to encourage members to take advantage of the various opportunities for training available to them. This was called the Mary Blakeman Bursary and the first recipient was Vicky Broad who attended the NODA Summer School at Loughborough University in August 2001.

21. Presidential Postscript

There has always been a President of the Newcastle Players, but what the person occupying the position did – or did not do – has varied somewhat. Broadly speaking there were three phases:

- From the beginning of the society until the late forties or early fifties the President was just a figurehead.

- In 1952 the office of Chairman was renamed President. Other than the change of name there was no change of function. The President continued to chair meetings of the Executive Committee and General Meetings of the society as the Chairman had done.

- In 1984 Bill Stevens, who had been President for the previous seven years, signified that he would like to be relieved of this heavy responsibility. The society agreed but, in gratitude for the services he had rendered, asked him to stay on as President, while reverting to the title of Chairman for the person who took over the executive functions.

The first President was Dr R A Keane FRCSI, a GP who had his surgery in Windsor House on the corner of Hanover Street in Newcastle, Pat Mason recalls. He was a friend of Pat's father and, like many members of the society in the early days, a member of the Catenian Association, a group of Catholic business and professional men with branches in a number of countries around the world.

"Dr Keane was only a figurehead," says Pat. "I don't remember him doing any of the menial tasks like putting out chairs in the hall before a performance or putting them away again afterwards."

By June 1936, when *The Barretts of Wimpole Street* was presented for one night at the Theatre Royal, Hanley in aid of the North Staffs. Royal Infirmary £20,000 Radium Appeal (after doing a regular four-night run at the Marsh Street Assembly Rooms the previous November), Dr Keane had acquired a Vice-President, Mr Alfred Denville MP, and when Dr Keane resigned as President in 1937 Mr Denville was asked if he would be President which he apparently agreed to do as there are various isolated references to him over the years from then until 1945.

What is puzzling is how Mr (later Sir Arthur) Denville came to be connected with the Newcastle Players. Research carried out by Rob Vaughan reveals that Alfred Arthur Hinchcliffe Denville J.P. was born in Nottingham of a theatrical family on 27th January 1876. He first appeared on stage as a babe in arms at the old Prince of Wales Theatre, Greenwich in a vintage melodrama of the time. His early life was spent travelling with his parents in the touring companies of which they were members. He attended Ushaw College, Durham, but he was soon back with his family, helping to supplement their slender income, and for several years toured with circus theatres. He later had various jobs before returning to the theatre starting the first and only repertoire in England at that time in Moriston in 1900. The same year he acquired the lease of a small theatre at Swansea.

In 1925 he bought Northwood Hall in Middlesex and dedicated it to the acting profession in memory of his son Jack who had died at the age of 26 after an injury on stage reactivated earlier damage sustained in the Great War. The hall was renamed Denville Hall and opened fully in 1926. It has since been extended and operates, as its website (www.denvillehall.org) states, as a "charity founded by actors and run by actors for the profession. It has been funded through the kindness of actors and theatre managers since 1925 . . . . It is available to people over 70 who have worked professionally as actors, from anywhere in the UK."

After several years' involvement in the theatre both as a manager and an actor Alfred Denville stood for parliament and unsuccessfully contested the Hanley Division of Stoke-on-Trent in 1928, which is perhaps where the North Staffordshire connection came in. Ironically when he did manage to become an MP it was representing not Newcastle-under-Lyme but the Central Division of Newcastle-upon-Tyne and he retained the seat until his retirement in 1945. A pioneer of the modern repertory theatre in the provinces and for many years known as "the actors' M.P." he died on March 23rd 1955 at the age of 79.

As mentioned earlier, the office of President in its present form came into being in 1984 when Bill Stevens decided to give up his executive duties. He was President from then until 1990. His successor was Ben Devall who served until his death in December 2001. Neither Bill nor Ben could be termed a mere figurehead. They both always present in the foyer of the Mitchell Memorial

Theatre whenever we performed there, ready to greet members and patrons alike. And they attended Executive Committee with great regularity and were thus on hand to give to give us the benefit of their wisdom and experience.

Even less of a figurehead is our current President, Elizabeth Rowley, who was elected to the position in 2002 after having been Chairman for the previous three years and Vice-Chairman for three years before that.

No person could be better fitted to be President of the Newcastle Players than Elizabeth (or Buffie as she is known on all but formal occasions). She has been in Newcastle Players all her life – and even longer. Her parents, John and Josephine were founder members of the society. As recorded elsewhere, John produced every play for the first ten years and he and Jo acted in many of them. Buffie's first stage non-appearance was in fact when her mother was acting in a play whilst pregnant with the new addition to the Rowley family who would later become our President.

Elizabeth Rowley

Buffie made her actual Newcastle Players debut in *Red Letter Day* at the Municipal Hall, Newcastle in November 1957. It was a small part of four lines, but it was the start of many more dramatic experiences. Over many years Buffie has taken several major parts, most notably the Mother Superior in *Letter from the General* (1970) and Princess Mary in *Crown Matrimonial* (1978). Her own very favourite part, however, was Mrs Soppit in J B Priestley's *When We Are Married* (1987).

Buffie says she was frequently admonished for writing her lines on any prop that was available: fans, knitting patterns, etc. or even on her hands when all else failed. But one incident that has become part of Newcastle Players folklore involved Buffie's inability (and everybody else's, it should be added) to understand Mary Blakeman's instruction to "follow your right hand round".

It ended up, as somebody once commented, "with Buffie screwing herself into the stage".

Like the rest of us, Buffie had to juggle her commitment to the society with the demands of her day job. Although, as she was a midwife, it would be better described in Buffie's case as a day and night job. As such, she worked for many years at the North Staffs Maternity Hospital. It was there that she became involved in Industrial Relations and after her retirement she continued lecturing in that subject.

Buffie says that, as her parents were so involved in Newcastle Players, her life grew around the society. The friendships thus formed have enhanced her life immeasurably and the society members and their families have become an integral part of her life. In recognition of her many years of service she was elected a Life Member of the society in 2003.

Appendix A

Meeting held in the Rehearsal Room Poole-field Avenue
Keele Road Newcastle on Sunday Feb. 14th. 1937 at 3-30 p.m.

Present.
Mr. Rowley,	Mrs. Wright,	Mrs. Hodnett,	Miss Griffiths,
Mr. Mason,	Miss Wright	Miss Tinsdill,	Miss D. McKnight
Mr. Tinsdill,	Miss U. Wright,	Mrs. Howard,	Miss Legge,
Mr. J. W. Wright,	Miss Brown,	Mrs. Rowley,	Mr. Connelly.

Proposition By Mr. Tinsdill, seconded by Miss Wright that a Dramatic Society be formed and that Foundation members consist of those present together with any old members of the old "Newcastle Players" who apply within one Month.
Resolution carried.

Proposed by Mr. Rowley and seconded by Mr. Tinsdill that Mr. Mason be appointed Chairman.
Resolution carried.

Proposed by Mrs. Wright seconded by Mrs. Hodnett, that Mr. Hand be appointed Vice- Chairman, and Mr. Walsh Secretary.
Resolution Carried.

Proposed by Miss Brown, and seconded by Mrs. Wright that Miss Connelly be appointed Treasurer.
Carried.

Proposed by Miss U. Wright and seconded by Miss Connelly that Miss D. McKnight be appointed Subscription Treasurer.
Resolution Carried.

Proposed by Mrs. Rowley and seconded by Miss D. McKnight that Mr. Rowley be appointed Producer.
Resolution carried.

Proposed by Miss Wright and seconded by Mrs. Howard that the Society admitted Catholics only as members, and Husbands and Wife's of Catholic members, who are non-Catholics.
Carried

Proposed by Mr. Wright and seconded by Mrs. Rowley that the newly formed society be named "The Newcastle Player" affiliated to the British Drama League.
Resolution carried.

Proposed by Mr. Tinsdill, and seconded by Miss Wright that the committee should consist of the following officers
Chairman, Vice Chairman, Secretary, Treasurer and four other members of the Society, and after a vote the following members were elected to serve on the Committee,
Mr. Connelly, Mr. Tinsdill, Miss Wright, Mr. Gunn.

Mr. Tinsdill proposed and Miss Wright seconded his proposal that Plays be selected and cast by the General Committee and that the selected play or plays are brought before the whole Society for consideration and final decision.
Resolution Carried.

Mr. Wright proposed and Miss U. Wright seconded his proposition that Dr. Keane be asked to be our President for one year.
Resolution carried.

Miss Brown proposed and Mr. Connelly seconded the proposition that a play be produced this season. Mr. Tinsdill proposed and Miss Wright seconded his proposition that the Society produced the "Two Mrs. Carrolls".
Both resolutions were carried.

Miss Tinsdill proposed and seconded by Miss Wright that the annual subscription to the society be 5/-

---

It was unanimously decided that all members of the old Society that were members of the newly formed Society, and had been elected to the Social Committee of the old society, were automatically members of the Social Committee of this Society.

Mr. Mason and Mr. Rowley kindly offered to jointly and severally guarantee an account to be opened at The Midland Bank, Hanley, up to £20 (Twenty Pounds.)

M Mason
21/3/37

Appendix B

40th Anniversary Party – 17 January 1975
John Barstow proposes the toast of The Newcastle Players

Ladies and Gentlemen, may I first say a very big thank you to you all for coming. We felt that the occasion of forty years warranted some recognition and it's my great pleasure to tell you that we have no less than two of our founder members here with us tonight. We're delighted about that and I'm quite sure that you will be.

I'm sorry I've got to refer to these notes but everybody knows that I never can remember what I've written or what I've seen printed. That's why I never get a part in a play.

Now, just a little bit of nostalgia. My association with the Newcastle Players doesn't go back quite to the first, but I can well remember Ernest Butterworth, the chairman on that occasion, who succeeded Jack Mason, who was the first chairman, when Sir Alfred Denville MP, a close friend of John Rowley, was the president. Now when Butterworth passed on, John Rowley asked John Legge if he would like to be chairman, but Sir Alfred Denville having also passed on, John Legge said he would certainly want to be president and president he was. For a long time. [In fact, John Legge was Chairman for four years before becoming President - GHP]

Whilst he was president I was secretary for some – this'll be contradicted in a minute – some fifteen years and I only stopped being secretary because of the executive committee's dislike of my dog. The reason for which I'm not going to tell you now. [laughter and indecipherable comments – GHP]

The Newcastle Players owe a lot to the early members and to their enthusiasm.

- John Rowley, the founder. He produced and he took the male lead. And good he was.

I think of a number of names:

- Denis Connelly who, as you all know – those who saw him – was professional standard on the stage without any doubt

- Pringle Brown

- Jack Mason

- Rose Moran – and Rose Moran, whom some of you will remember, saw the little note in *The Sentinel* tonight and she had the grace to ring up somebody here and she said she hoped we'd have a nice time.

And I hope we have a nice time. There are other names I think of:

- Eluned Mason. How grateful we should be to her for unfailing generosity about props and furniture when we were short.

- Bill Stevens and his great dependability. If Bill says he'll be there at seven o'clock to do a job, you can bet your bottom dollar that at seven clock he's there and he does the job. That's the sort of enthusiasm that this little society is so proud of.

Now, since those early days, quite a lot of things have contributed to our continued success.

- We all know Mary B's contribution and how she has inspired potential producers. That is proved already and will be again. That's something, you know, that we must be proud of. We are proud of.

- And not a little of our success is perhaps due – or, shall I say, is due – to our present Hon Sec. For his – I don't quite know what to call it – for his knack, I think, in getting minutes right. And his regular bulletins. How much we enjoy them.

I'm anxious not to labour things too much, but I would stress our past and how much, these days, our older members value it. And how delighted we are to know that the present younger members are as keen and as enthusiastic as were the early Players. And how much it is hoped that they – in another forty years – and that's a long time – will be able to look back with the same amount of pleasure that we older members are experiencing at this moment.

I have said, perhaps ad nauseam, that we are a nice society, so I ask you to be upstanding and the toast is: "The Newcastle Players".

[Bill Stevens's voice] "May they go from strength to strength."

Enid Tunstill responds to the toast of The Newcastle Players

Mr President and fellow members, I am very honoured to have been asked to reply to the toast this evening, on this auspicious occasion and, unaccustomed as I am to public speaking, I shall strive manfully, if that is the word, to overcome my natural [Bill Stevens's voice: "womanly"] shyness – oh, all right, womanfully, then – to overcome my natural shyness.

But, putting flippancy and fun aside for a moment, I make no apology for – not sentimentality – but for the sincerity of the sentiment I feel for the Newcastle Players.

I would suggest to you that there are not many societies like ours. In the Players we have something unique, due in great part to the active feeling of goodwill towards the society and to all the individual members who comprise it from the individual members of the society. That we are individuals can be in no doubt. That is why we join a dramatic society. But we are individuals with a common interest and a common purpose. And therein lies our strength. For strong we are.

There is a bond between the Players – particularly at the present time – and it is something that should be valued very highly, because it cannot be brought about by wishing or willing. It must come, like true discipline, from within. It's not easily come by and it shouldn't be easily let go. It should be guarded jealously with all the awareness we have at our command.

As our President so rightly said, we owe our existence to the enthusiasm of the original members of the society and to our founder, John Rowley. And to their faith in the project that they started. And our continued existence – and let's not call it existence, because it's a life – to the Players who followed on and are following on. And, god willing, our future existence to the very youngest members and the ones who are not old enough to join but are waiting at the door to come in.

It's a most pleasing and satisfying thing to have one's children follow on with enthusiasm into the society, as many of us, thankfully, can testify.

But, if all this sounds serious and solemn, you know that's not the whole story. You know, none better, that we have fun and warmth and true fellowship. We are, as our President has said so many times, a nice society. And it follows that we are nice people. We are always ready to share our heritage with new members who come along. If they are our kind of people, then they integrate and become a part of us in no time at all. If not – and it's nothing to their discredit – although nothing is ever said, they fall away and leave us with, for us, only the best. And that makes for great solidarity and again that strength, which our erstwhile President John Legge was always urging us to go from and to.

One of the nicest and, these days, most remarkable things about the Players is the absolute lack of that much publicised "age gap". At least, I've never felt it. I feel as young – and as daft – as the most youthful of our tribe. I only hope it doesn't cut both ways and they feel as old as I am.

But I'm sure the Players have the secret of eternal youth for it is, after all, all in the mind. I'm very proud to be a member. I'm eternally grateful. And I'm sure that we all feel so. I tell you, if there's no Newcastle Players in heaven, I don't want to go.

And so, I thank you Mr President for your toast, for the great spirit and all that it stands for. For this forty year old family of the Newcastle Players. That *Dear Octopus* from whose tentacles we never quite escape. And never really want to.

Transcribed by Geoff Price (GHP), December 2005

Appendix C

Newcastle Players Members (September 2006)

Ruth Alexander	Lucy Garner	Barbara Massey
Michelle Baskeyfield	June Godfrey	Claire McGregor
Eric Beardmore	Mick Gould	Charles Miller
Lesley Benyon	Val Grieve	Ray Miller
Terry Benyon	Vic Grieve	Simon Milward
Jill Bowdery	Chris Hammond	Annie Morris
Maggie Brady	Moira Hammond	John Owens
Vicky Broad	**Ann Haycock**	Val Owens
Lucy Bryan	Alan Hodgkinson	Vi Pointon
Patrick Buckley	Yvonne Holford	Gill Pollard
Andy Clayton	John Hough	Joy Pownall
Margaret Davies	Melissa Humphries	**Geoff Price**
Lara De-Leuw	Ann Hurlstone	Mary Price
Margaret Devall	Joy Jackson	Judith Robinson
Gareth Dowson	Margaret Johnson	**Elizabeth Rowley**
Anna Drinkwater	Alan Jones	Shane Saunders
Olive Dunn	James Lawton	Kay Scott
Mike Egan	Eileen Leedham	Judy Scott
Helen Farrington	Tina Leek	Kay Sewell
Jonathan Fernyhough	Aline Lewis	Rob Sewell
Sheila Fernyhough	Kate Lindsay	Pam Shufflebotham
Sylvia Fisher	Catherine Lovatt	Carol Simmonds
Sue Ford	Janet Mason	Harvey Simmonds
Martin Frain	**Pat Mason**	Richard Slater
Enid Frieder	Wyn Mason	Maureen Stevens

Richard Stevens	Alan Wagg	Bob West
Vida Stevens	Janet Wagg	Di West
John Stone	June Wallbank	Judith Whewell
Pat Sunderland	Christine Ward	John Whittaker
Helen Thomas	Jim Ward	Pat Whittaker
Amanda Tilsley	John Wardle	Chris Wilkinson
Janet Vaughan	Joyce Wardle	Tom Williamson
Robert Vaughan	Maureen Watson	

Notes:

1. The members whose names are in bold type are Life Members of the society.

2. Ann Haycock and Janet Vaughan use their maiden names (Ann McArdle and Janet Mulliner) for stage purposes.

Appendix D

Photo Credits

Photographs in this book, unless otherwise credited below, are by the author.

Chapter 1:
The cast of *"The Barretts of Wimpole Street"* (source unknown).

Chapter 2:
"Nine Till Six" and *"No Medals"* (probably Staffordshire Sentinel)
"Viceroy Sarah" (Staffordshire Sentinel)
Municipal Hall on pages 13 and 14 (Borough Museum and Art Gallery, Newcastle-under-Lyme)

Chapter 3:
"The House by the Lake" and *"Celebration"* (Staffordshire Sentinel)

Chapter 4:
"I Have Five Daughters", *"Another Language"*, *"The Blue Goose"*, *"Castle in the Air"*, *"Spider's Web"* and *"Suddenly at Home"* (Staffordshire Sentinel)
"Hobson's Choice" and *"The Ghost Train"* (Robert Vaughan)

Chapter 7:
Lower Street Chapel (Borough Museum and Art Gallery, Newcastle-under-Lyme)
18 West View (Staffordshire Sentinel)

Chapter 10:
21st Birthday cake (source unknown)
Silver Jubilee and *"Outside Edge"* (Staffordshire Sentinel)
40th Anniversary (Paul Tunstill)
Seventieth Anniversary (Robert Vaughan)

Chapter 11:
40th Anniversary (Paul Tunstill)

Chapter 14:
"Outside Edge" (Richard Price)

Chapter 18:
John Barstow (Staffordshire Sentinel)
John Rowley (probably Staffordshire Sentinel)

Chapter 19:
"The Archers" (BBC)
Hilary Tindall (probably Staffordshire Sentinel)
Photographs of Geoffrey Saunders, Tom Farrington and Simon Milward supplied by themselves

Chapter 20:
Breath of Life presentation (Chris Hammond)

Rear Cover:
Geoff Price (Rebecca Ashley)